COLLECTIONS

Intervention Reader
Teacher's Guide

Grade 2

D1524953

Harcourt

Orlando   Boston   Dallas   Chicago   San Diego

Visit *The Learning Site!*
www.harcourtschool.com

ISBN 0-15-312742-2

4 5 6 7 8 9 10 082 2002 2001

Contents

O nce upon a time, there was a town whose playground was at the edge of a cliff. Every so often, a child would fall off the cliff. Finally the town council decided something should be done about the serious injuries to children . . . Some council members wanted to put a fence at the top of the cliff, but others wanted to put an ambulance at the bottom.

Dr. Robert E. Slavin,
Educational Leadership, February 1996

Introduction

During the past few decades, increasing amounts of energy and funding have gone into remedial programs for students experiencing difficulty in learning to read and write. Yet students who spend several years in such programs during the elementary grades often enter middle school far behind grade-level expectations. Research shows clearly that remediation is not doing the job. In recent years, in fact, it has shown that using intervention strategies is a much more promising answer.

What Are "Intervention Strategies"?

Intervention strategies are the fences we build to protect those students who may experience some perilous "cliffs" no matter how well we have planned our curriculum. These strategies offer support and guidance to the student who is struggling. The strategies themselves are no mystery. They are based on the same time-honored techniques that effective teachers have used for years— teaching students on their instructional reading level, modeling previewing and predicting, conducting guided reading, and giving direct instruction in strategic reading, vocabulary, phonics, and structural analysis skills.

> "Intervention is less costly than years of remediation, less costly than retention, and—ultimately—less costly to children's self-esteem."
>
> **Dr. Dorothy Strickland**

Intervention works best in conjunction with a strong core program. Instructional techniques should focus on specific needs of students, as determined by systematic monitoring of progress. Here is what the research says about the components of an effective intervention program:

Materials

- It is essential that students read texts with which they are successful. Effective intervention strategies can widen the variety of texts accessible to students, but it is also important to provide reading material at children's instructional reading level.

- Guiding students who need extra support through a preview of the literature, with attention to important vocabulary, will help ensure success when materials are challenging.

Instruction

- Successful intervention programs allow students to spend more time reading and responding to texts at their instructional reading level. Children are also taught when and how to use reading skills and strategies.

- Teachers should observe any problems students have during activities and use flexible grouping to provide more individualized instruction for those who need additional help.

- Phonics and structural analysis skills must be given strong, systematic treatment. They should be taught along with strategies for discovering word meaning, which is an equally important word identification skill.

Using the
Intervention Readers
and *Intervention Reader*
Teacher's Guides

The goal of the ***Collections*** *Intervention Readers* and the *Teacher's Guides* is to provide the scaffolding, extra support, and extra reading practice that below-level readers need to succeed in the mainstream reading program—without excluding them from the instruction their classmates receive.

Intervention Readers

Intervention Readers are student editions that are designed specifically to help struggling readers. The easy-to-read selections in the *Intervention Readers*—

- are consistently parallel in genre, theme, and content to the corresponding selections in the ***Collections*** Student Editions.

- are written on a level that more closely approximates the struggling reader's instructional reading level.

- gradually increase in difficulty, so that by the end of the book, students are reading on-grade-level material.

- systematically apply high-frequency words, ***Collections*** vocabulary, and basic phonics skills.

Each *Intervention Reader* selection is accompanied by a **Student Response Page** and—when a Skill Lesson accompanies the corresponding ***Collections*** selection—a parallel **Skill Lesson**, written with the same vocabulary and on the same reading level as the rest of the *Intervention Reader* selections.

Teacher's Guides

Intervention Reader Teacher's Guides give step-by-step support in using the *Intervention Reader*, in conjunction with **Collections**, to provide comprehensive support for below-level readers. There is one *Intervention Reader* lesson to correspond with each lesson plan in the **Collections** Teacher's Edition.

Each *Intervention Reader Teacher's Guide* lesson includes the following resources:

- **Phonics/Decoding Lesson** preteaches basic phonics and word analysis skills essential for reading. Each skill is systematically applied in the corresponding *Intervention Reader* selection and reviewed in subsequent selections.

- **Phonics Reproducible Student Activity Page** reinforces the Phonics/Word Analysis Skill Lesson. This page can be used as a teacher-directed or independent activity.

- **Introducing Vocabulary** activity teaches additional important vocabulary that appears in the corresponding **Collections** Student Edition selection and in the *Intervention Reader* selection. This extra vocabulary instruction bolsters children's chances of reading each piece successfully.

- **Vocabulary Reproducible Student Activity Page** gives children an opportunity to use the *Intervention Reader* vocabulary in context and show their understanding of it. It also provides a preview of the upcoming *Intervention Reader* selection. The teacher can guide children through the page, or children can complete the page independently while the teacher works with other groups.

- **Directed Reading Lesson** provides additional scaffolding for successfully reading the *Intervention Reader* selection. The lesson offers suggestions for dividing the selection into cohesive sections that are manageable for children, and then using a variety of techniques to help children read these sections successfully.

- **Student Response Reproducible Student Activity Page** gives children an opportunity to respond to the *Intervention Reader* selection and show that they have understood it. It also provides further reinforcement of the *Intervention Reader* vocabulary.

Consonant Review

Review of Initial and Final Consonants

Teach/Model

IDENTIFY THE SOUND Read the following sentence: *Sam ran to get a fan.* Ask children to repeat the sentence three times, listening carefully for the sound each word begins with. Then ask these questions, repeating the sentence as necessary: *Which word begins with the /s/ sound in* sack*? (Sam) Which word begins with the /f/ sound in* far*? (fan) Which word begins with the /g/ sound in* game*? (get) Which word begins with the /r/ sound in* round*? (ran) Which word begins with the /t/ sound in* tip*? (to)*

ASSOCIATE LETTERS TO THEIR SOUNDS Write the following consonants on the board, omitting the items in parentheses:

b	c (/k/)	d	f	g (/g/)	h	j
k	l	m	n	p	qu	r
s	t	v	w	x (final)	y (initial)	z

Remind children that these letters are called *consonants.* Point to *qu* and tell children that the consonant *q* is almost always followed by the vowel *u,* and that *qu* almost always stands for the /kw/ sound. Then follow this procedure for each consonant: Point to the consonant, say its name aloud, and have children repeat it. Ask: *Which word begins with the /b/ sound in* back—*can or* bin*? (bin) Who can think of another word that starts with the /b/ sound?* Give several children the opportunity to respond. Point out that *c* and *k* both can stand for the /k/ sound. If some children say that *kite* begins like *can* or that *car* begins like *kite,* tell them that they have identified the right sound, but a different letter stands for the sound in the word(s) they suggested. For *x,* ask: *Which word ends with the sound you hear at the end of* mix—*bat or* ax*? (ax)*

Practice/Apply

APPLY THE SKILL Consonant Substitution Write the words in the first row below on the board. Read each word aloud and have children repeat it. Then make the changes necessary to form the words in parentheses. After substituting each initial consonant, have a volunteer read the new word aloud. Try to give each child an opportunity to respond.

tan	mat	sad	ham
(m)an	(c)at	(b)ad	(P)am
(f)an	(b)at	(m)ad	(j)am
(c)an	(s)at	(f)ad	(S)am
(p)an	(f)at	(p)ad	

To give children practice with final consonants, follow the same procedure using these words:

sad	mad	ham	tap
sa(t)	ma(n)	ha(t)	ta(n)
Sa(m)	ma(t)	ha(d)	ta(x)

DICTATION AND WRITING Tell children to number their papers 1–10. Explain that you will say ten words and that, after you say each word, they should write the consonant the word begins with. After each consonant is written, write it on the board so children can check their work. They should draw a line through each incorrect consonant and write the correct one above it.

1. tap (t)	2. map (m)	3. ran (r)	4. sack (s)	5. bad (b)
6. fan (f)	7. pat (p)	8. lamb (l)	9. dad (d)	10. nap (n)

PROVIDE INDEPENDENT PRACTICE Have each child create an ABC book of consonants. To do this, they should write each consonant at the top of a separate sheet of paper and then draw a picture of something that begins with the sound that letter stands for. (You may need to provide help with *c*, *k*, and *qu*. Remind children that they should draw a picture of something that ends in *x*.)

For additional reinforcement of each consonant sound/letter relationship, have children use the *Phonics Express* CD-ROM.

Phonics

The Loud Ride

by Susan McCloskey   **Use with *Blue Skies*, pages 6–13.**

Preteaching Skills: Short Vowel /a/a

Teach/Model

IDENTIFY THE SOUND Read aloud the following sentence: *The cat sat on Dan's lap.* Ask children to repeat the sentence three times, listening for words that have the /a/ sound. Have children identify the words in the sentence that have the /a/ sound. (*cat, sat, Dan's, lap*) Ask children to raise their hands each time they hear a word with the /a/ sound: *cab, tip, tap, ran, lock, win, sad.*

ASSOCIATE LETTERS TO THEIR SOUNDS Write the sentence *The cat sat on Dan's lap* on the board, and have a volunteer underline the words that contain the letter *a*. Tell children that in these words, the letter *a* stands for the /a/ sound. Have children read the underlined words with you.

WORD BLENDING Write the words *cab, tap, ran,* and *sad* on the board and underline the *a* in each. Model reading the word *cab* by blending the sounds the letters stand for: Slide your hand under the letters as you slowly elongate the sounds /ccaabb/. Then read the word naturally—*cab.* Have children do the same. Have children take turns blending the sounds in each remaining word and reading them aloud.

Practice/Apply

APPLY THE SKILL *Consonant Substitution* Write on the board the words *cab* and *ran.* Tell children that once they can read a word such as *cab* or *ran,* they can read many other words that end the same way. Model consonant substitution by erasing the *c* in *cab* and writing a *t* to form *tab.* Then replace the *r* in *ran* with *m* to form *man.* Replace other initial consonants as shown to form new words that have the /a/ sound. Ask volunteers to take turns reading aloud each new word in parentheses.

ran (man)   sad (mad)   pat (bat)
fan (pan)   pad (had)   sat (cat)

DICTATION AND WRITING Tell children to number their papers 1–8. Dictate the following words, and have children write them. After each word is written, write it on the board so children can proofread their work. They should draw a line through a misspelled word and write the correct spelling below it.

1. can*	2. man	3. pat	4. bad*	*Word appears in
5. sad	6. mad*	7. mat	8. bat	"The Loud Ride."

READ LONGER WORDS *Ending -s* On the board, write the word *cats.* Tell children that they can often figure out a new word by first looking for a part they know. Cover the *s* in *cats* with your hand, and ask a volunteer to read *cat.* Model how to blend the word *cat.* Slide your hand under the letters *ca* as you slowly elongate the sounds /ccaa/. Add the *t,* and have children slowly blend the sounds with you. Then read the word *cat* naturally, and ask children to do the same. Have children add the /s/ sound to read the word *cats.* Follow the same procedure with the word *hats.* Then ask children to read aloud the words *bats, fans,* and *caps* and explain how they figured them out.

REPRODUCIBLE STUDENT ACTIVITY PAGE

INDEPENDENT PRACTICE See the reproducible Student Activity on page 3.

The Loud Ride

Write the word that best completes each sentence.

cat	pan	bat	van	hat	sad

1. My _____ is in my lap.

2. The jam is in the _____.

3. Pam has a _____.

4. This man is not _____.

5. That _____ had a nap.

6. A cat is in that _____ !

Introducing Vocabulary

Apply word identification strategies.

IDENTIFY VOCABULARY WORDS Write the vocabulary words on the board, and ask volunteers to identify any they know. Then read each word aloud and have children say them after you. Repeat this procedure several times. Remind children that they know the sounds many letters stand for. Explain that thinking about the letters and sounds they know can help them read new words. Have children use their knowledge of the sounds letters stand for and the clues you give them to recognize words. Give them the following clues and have a volunteer say and frame the word that answers each one.

VOCABULARY DEFINED
book printed sheets of paper bound together on one side
knew was sure of; past tense of *know*
never at no time; not ever
noisy loud
reading getting the meaning of printed material by looking at printed words and understanding them
story a telling of events

This means you were sure about something. (*knew*) This is something you would find in a library. (*book*) This is what people are doing when they are looking at a book. (*reading*) You might have one of these read to you at bedtime. (*story*) This word means the same as *loud*. (*noisy*) This means "not ever." (*never*)

Check understanding.

Ask children to write the vocabulary words on a sheet of paper. Then ask the following questions. After children name the correct word, they should circle that word on their papers.

- **When you tell about something that happened, what are you telling?** (*story*)
- **What word would you use to tell someone that you were sure of something?** (*knew*)
- **What word would you use to tell about something that was not quiet?** (*noisy*)
- **What would you find in the library?** (*book*)
- **What are you doing when you figure out words you see in a book?** (*reading*)
- **What word means "at no time"?** (*never*)

Children may be unfamiliar with some of the words in the title of the selection they are about to read. After distributing the vocabulary page, point to the title, "The Loud Ride," read it aloud, and have children read it with you.

REPRODUCIBLE STUDENT ACTIVITY PAGE

INDEPENDENT PRACTICE See the reproducible Student Activity on page 5.

NOTE: The following vocabulary words from "Lucy's Quiet Book" are reinforced in "The Loud Ride." If children are unfamiliar with these words, point them out as you encounter them during reading: *loud* (p. 6); *wonder* (p. 9); *angry* (p. 10); *idea*, *grinned* (p. 11); and *surprised* (p. 12).

Name _____

The Loud Ride

Read each sentence. Write the word from the box that makes sense in the sentence.

never	knew	book	reading	story	noisy

1. "What are you _____?" said Dad.

2. "I am reading this big _____," said Jan.

3. "I _____ that," said Dad.

4. "How come it is so _____?" he said.

5. "I am reading a noisy _____ in this book," said Jan.

6. "I _____ knew a book could be noisy," said Dad. "I like it!"

Directed Reading

Page 6 Point to each word in the title as you read it aloud. Then ask children to repeat it. Ask a volunteer to describe the picture on page 6. Explain that the man driving is the father of the two girls and one boy in the van. Tell children that the girl who is reading is Jan. Then have children read page 6 and ask: **What is special about the story Jan is reading?** (Possible response: *It is loud.*) INFERENTIAL: IMPORTANT DETAILS Then model the thinking: **Dad says he never knew a book could be so loud.** LITERAL: NOTE DETAILS

Page 7 Have a volunteer read aloud the first line on page 7, and ask children what they think Sam is doing. Have them read the rest of the page to find out. **What is Sam doing?** (Possible response: *He is reading a book, too.*) LITERAL: NOTE DETAILS Model the thinking: **Jan and Sam are reading noisy books. Jan's book says, "TAP! TAP, TAP!" and Sam's book says, "RAP! RAP, RAP!"** INFERENTIAL: COMPARE AND CONTRAST

Page 8 Ask a volunteer to read aloud the first line on page 8. Then ask children if they think Pam has a noisy book, too. Have them read the rest of the page to find out. **What is Pam's book like?** (*It is noisy.*) LITERAL: CONFIRM PREDICTIONS **How does Pam feel about the story she is reading?** (*She likes it.*) LITERAL: NOTE DETAILS

Page 9 Ask children why they think the van has stopped. Then have them read page 9. Children may need help reading the word *wonder* in the last sentence. Discuss its meaning with them. **Why has the van stopped?** (*There is a herd of sheep blocking the road.*) INFERENTIAL: CAUSE AND EFFECT **What do you think the characters will do next?** (Possible response: *Dad will honk the horn to get the sheep to move.*) INFERENTIAL: MAKE PREDICTIONS

Page 10 Ask children to look at the picture on page 10. Explain that the family is figuring out what to do next. Point to the word *angry* and read it aloud. Ask children what *angry* means. Repeat the procedure with the word *idea*. Then have children read page 10 to find out who has an idea. **Who has an idea?** (*Jan, Sam, and Pam*) LITERAL: NOTE DETAILS **What word on this page means the same as *angry*?** (*mad*) INFERENTIAL: RECOGNIZE SYNONYMS

Page 11 Have children read page 11 to see whether they can find out what the idea is. Model the thinking: **I don't know what the idea is, but Dad likes it. He grins and says it is not a bad idea.** INFERENTIAL: SPECULATE

Page 12 Ask children to use the picture to guess what the idea is. Then have them read page 12 to find out. **What did Jan, Sam, and Pam do to get the sheep to move?** (Possible response: *They read their books in a loud voice.*) INFERENTIAL: CAUSE AND EFFECT

SUMMARIZING THE SELECTION Ask children to think about what happened at the beginning, middle, and end of "The Loud Ride." Help them summarize the story in three or four sentences.

Answers to Think About It Questions

Page 13
1. They read from their noisy books. SUMMARY
2. He thought that books were not noisy. INTERPRETATION
3. Accept reasonable responses. TASK

Name _____

The Loud Ride

Fill in the story map to tell about what happened in "The Loud Ride." Use the story words in the boxes to help you.

| van | Setting |

| Characters |

| never reading | Beginning | knew books noisy |

Jan, Sam, and Pam are _____.

Dad said, "_____."

| road sheep | Middle |

The van stops because _____

_____.

| loud stories read | End |

Jan, Pam, and Sam _____

_____.

A Walk in the Woods

by Barbara Diaz   **Use with *Blue Skies*, pages 14–21.**

Preteaching Skills: Short Vowel /i/i

Teach/Model

IDENTIFY THE SOUND Ask children to repeat the following sentence aloud three times: *Did Tim win that pin and that hat?* Have children identify the words that have the /i/ sound. (*Did, Tim, win, pin*)

ASSOCIATE LETTERS TO THEIR SOUNDS Write *Did Tim win that pin and that hat?* on the board. Ask a volunteer to underline the words that contain the letter *i*. Tell children that in these words, the *i* stands for the /i/ sound. Have children read the underlined words with you.

WORD BLENDING Write the words *fin, tin, bin, Kim,* and *him* on the board. Underline the *i* in each. Model reading the word *fin* by blending the sounds the letters stand for: Slide your hand under the letters as you slowly elongate /ffiinn/. Then read the word naturally. Have children do the same. Have children take turns blending the sounds in each remaining word and reading them aloud. Then model replacing initial consonants to make these words: *fin, tin, bin; Kim, him, dim.* Have children blend the sounds to read each new word.

Practice/Apply

APPLY THE SKILL *Vowel Substitution* Write the first word in each pair below on the board, and have children read them. Model vowel substitution by erasing the *a* in *tan* and writing an *i* to form *tin*. Make the changes necessary to form the word in parentheses. Have volunteers take turns reading each new word aloud.

tan (tin)   tip (tap)   pan (pin)   bit (bat)   sat (sit)   lap (lip)

Discuss this generalization about short vowel sounds: When a vowel is in between two consonants in a word, the word usually has a short vowel sound.

DICTATION AND WRITING Have children number a sheet of paper 1–8. Dictate the following words, and have children write them. After each word is written, write it on the board so children can proofread their work. They should draw a line through a misspelled word and write the correct spelling below it.

1. pin   2. lip   3. sit*   4. sip
5. tin   6. did*   7. bit*   8. fit

*Word appears in "A Walk in the Woods."

READ LONGER WORDS *Ending -ing; Two-Syllable Words* Explain that a *syllable* is a word part that has one vowel sound. Clap your hands once as you say *sit*. Explain that *sit* has one syllable. Then clap your hands twice as you say *sitting*. Explain that *sitting* has two syllables, *sit* and *ting*. Have children clap out the syllables as you say these words: *tip, tipping, win, winning, bat, batting.* Then write *sitting* on the board and ask a volunteer to underline *sit*. Explain that when the ending *-ing* is added to a word that has a vowel in between two consonants, the final consonant is usually doubled. Write the word *tipping* on the board and read it aloud. Ask which part of the word says *tip* and which part says *ping*. Ask what *tip* and *ping* together say. Have children blend the word parts to read *tipping*. Repeat this procedure with *winning* and *batting*.

REPRODUCIBLE STUDENT ACTIVITY PAGE

....

INDEPENDENT PRACTICE See the reproducible Student Activity on page 9.

Name _____

A Walk in the Woods

Fill in the oval in front of the sentence that tells about the picture.

1 ◯ My cat hid in the bin.
   ◯ Tim did find his bat.
   ◯ The cat sits in his lap.

2 ◯ She is sitting with her bat.
   ◯ She is sitting in a van.
   ◯ She is hitting now.

3 ◯ Is that a pig in the van?
   ◯ That pig is so big!
   ◯ I see a pig in a wig.

4 ◯ Tim finds a pin in the tin.
   ◯ Is the wig in the tin?
   ◯ All my hats are in the tin.

5 ◯ She did win a bat.
   ◯ She did win a pin.
   ◯ She is in the van.

6 ◯ This fits him.
   ◯ This is big for him.
   ◯ He is sitting down.

Introducing Vocabulary

USE SOUND-LETTER CORRESPONDENCES Write the vocabulary words on the board, and ask volunteers to identify any they know. Then read each word aloud and have children say them after you. Repeat the procedure several times. Remind children that thinking about the letters and sounds they know can help them read new words. Have children use their knowledge of the sounds that letters stand for and the clues you give them to recognize words. Give them the following clues and have a volunteer say and frame the word that answers each one: red and round fruits (*apples*); tall plants that people sometimes climb (*trees*); something thin and green you find on trees (*leaves*); a time of year when leaves turn red and orange (*fall*); short trips you can take on foot (*walks*); liked a lot (*loved*).

VOCABULARY DEFINED
apples round, crunchy fruits that can be red, yellow, or green
fall season of the year between summer and winter
leaves flat, thin, green parts of a plant or tree
loved felt a deep affection for someone or something
trees tall plants with wooden trunks and leaves
walks trips taken on foot; strolls

Ask children to write the vocabulary words on a sheet of paper. Then ask the following questions. After children name the correct word, they should circle it on their papers.

- **What word means "trips taken on foot"?** *(walks)*
- **What fruit might you put in a pie?** *(apples)*
- **What do apples grow on?** *(trees)*
- **What do you call the flat, green things that grow on trees?** *(leaves)*
- **What season comes after summer?** *(fall)*
- **What word names what you felt about someone special?** *(loved)*

Children may be unfamiliar with some of the words in the title of the selection they are about to read. After distributing the vocabulary page, point to the title, "A Walk in the Woods," read it aloud, and have children read it with you.

NOTE: The following vocabulary words from "Henry and Mudge Under the Yellow Moon" are reinforced in "A Walk in the Woods." If children are unfamiliar with these words, point them out as you encounter them during reading: *woods* (p. 14); *sniffing* (p. 15); *south, picked,* and *chipmunks* (p. 16).

Name _____

A Walk in the Woods

Read the ad.

Come See the Trees This Fall!

It is **fall.** Come to Big Trees Park!

What can you do there? You can go for **walks.** You can look up at the big **trees.** You can see the **leaves** come down. You can find **apples** in the trees. If you like, you can pick some apples. Kim said she **loved** her visit to Big Trees Park. So will you.

Come for a visit now!

Complete each sentence by writing a word from the ad above. Choose from the words in dark type.

1. The ad said to come to Big Trees Park in the _____.

2. The _____ come down in the fall.

3. The ad said you can pick some _____.

4. You can find the apples up in the _____.

5. You can go for _____ in Big Trees Park.

6. Kim said she _____ her visit to Big Trees Park.

Directed Reading

Pages 14–15 Ask a volunteer to read aloud the title of the story. Then ask children to describe the characters and setting. Then have them predict what the girl and dog love to do on a walk in the woods. Have children read pages 14 and 15 to confirm their predictions. **What does the girl like about walking in the woods?** (*walking in the fall leaves*) LITERAL: NOTE DETAILS **What does the dog like?** (*sniffing the leaves*) LITERAL: NOTE DETAILS **How are Kim's experience and Tip's experience in the woods alike? How are they different?** (Possible response: *They are alike because they both love the woods in the fall. They are different because Kim loves walking in the leaves but Tip loves sniffing them.*) INFERENTIAL: COMPARE AND CONTRAST

Page 16 Discuss the illustration on pages 16 and 17 with children and ask what they think Tip is looking for. Have them read the rest of the page to find out. **What is Tip looking for?** (*chipmunks*) LITERAL: NOTE DETAILS **Is this what you thought he was looking for?** (Responses will vary.) INFERENTIAL: CONFIRM PREDICTIONS

Page 17 Ask children to predict whether Kim and Tip will follow the chipmunk. Have them read page 17 to find out. **Will Kim and Tip follow the chipmunk?** (*yes*) INFERENTIAL: MAKE PREDICTIONS **How do you know?** (*because Kim asks, "Can you find his tree?"*) METACOGNITIVE: DRAW CONCLUSIONS

Page 18 Have children describe what has happened in the illustration on page 18. Then have them read the page to find out what the chipmunk will do. **Does the chipmunk come down from the tree?** (*no*) LITERAL: NOTE DETAILS **Why do you think the chipmunk does not come down?** (Possible response: *It is probably afraid of Tip.*) INFERENTIAL: CAUSE AND EFFECT

Page 19 Ask children to describe the picture on page 19. **What does Kim have in her pockets?** (*apples*) **How can you tell?** (*Her pockets are full and she says she loves picking apples.*) METACOGNITIVE: DRAW CONCLUSIONS

Have children read page 19 to find out how the story ends. **How does the story end?** (Possible response: *Kim and Tip have to go home.*) INFERENTIAL: SEQUENCE **Did Kim and Tip have a good time on their walk? How do you know?** (*Yes, because Kim says that she and Tip loved the things they did and saw.*) METACOGNITIVE: DRAW CONCLUSIONS

SUMMARIZING THE SELECTION Ask children to work in small groups and summarize the story by acting it out. They might use crumpled balls of paper for apples. One child can play Kim talking to Tip, and another can describe the walk in the woods. INFERENTIAL: SUMMARIZE

Answers to Think About It Questions

Page 20 Read the page with children and have them discuss their responses to items 1 and 2. For the last item, brainstorm ideas with children before they begin to write. Possible responses for items 1–3 are shown below.

1. Kim and Tip loved to take walks in the woods. They watched a chipmunk in its tree. SUMMARY
2. It may be afraid. INTERPRETATION
3. Accept reasonable responses. TASK

Page 21 For instruction on the Focus Skill: Setting, see page 21 in *Blue Skies*.

A Walk in the Woods

Complete the story strip to show what happened in "A Walk in the Woods."

When do Kim and Tip like to go for walks? _____ _____	Where do Kim and Tip like to go for walks? _____ _____
Who loves sniffing the leaves? _____ _____	Who loves the apples in the trees? _____ _____
What animal do Kim and Tip see? _____ _____	What if you could go for a walk in the woods? What would you like to see there? _____ _____ _____

Phonics

One Fine Night

by Jean Groce   Use with *Blue Skies*, pages 22–29.

Preteaching Skills: Vowel Variant /ôl/*all*

Teach/Model

IDENTIFY THE SOUND Ask children to repeat the following sentence aloud several times: *All the balls hit the wall.* Have children identify the words that have the /ôl/ sound. (*all, balls, wall*)

ASSOCIATE LETTERS TO THEIR SOUNDS Write on the board the sentence *All the balls hit the wall.* Ask a volunteer to underline words that contain the letters *all.* Tell children that in these words, the letters *all* stand for the /ôl/ sound. Read the following words aloud, and ask children to raise their hands each time they hear a word with the /ôl/ sound: *can, call, ball, bat, fit, fall, his, hall.*

WORD BLENDING Write the words *call, ball, fall,* and *hall* on the board and underline the *all* in each. Model reading the word *call* by blending the sounds the letters stand for: Slide your hand under the letters as you slowly elongate the sounds /kkôôll/. Then read *call* naturally and have children repeat it. Have volunteers take turns blending the sounds in the remaining words and reading them aloud.

Practice/Apply

APPLY THE SKILL *Consonant Substitution* Tell children that once they can read the word *call,* they can read many other words that end in *all.* Write on the board the word *call* and model replacing the *c* in *call* with *b* to form *ball.* Then replace the *b* in *ball* to form *fall.* Continue replacing the initial consonant as shown below to form new words that have the /ôl/ sound. Have children take turns reading each new word aloud.

call   ball   fall   hall   mall   wall   tall

DICTATION AND WRITING Ask children to number their papers 1–7. Write *tall* on the board and tell children that all of the words you will say will rhyme with *tall* and will have the same spelling pattern for the /ôl/ sound. Dictate the following words, and have children write them. After each word is written, write it on the board so children can proofread their work. Children should draw a line through a misspelled word and write the correct spelling below it.

1. ball   2. fall   3. hall   4. all*
5. call*   6. wall   7. mall

*Word appears in "One Fine Night."

Then dictate the following sentence: *That bat will fall.*

READ LONGER WORDS *Word Endings* Write the following words on the board: *calling, malls, falling, halls.* Remind children that they should look for words they know in longer words. Point to *calling* and read it aloud. Ask children which part of the word says *call* and which part says *ing.* Ask children what *call* and *ing* together say. Have children blend the word parts to form the longer word *calling.* Repeat this procedure with each word on the board.

REPRODUCIBLE STUDENT ACTIVITY PAGE
....
INDEPENDENT PRACTICE See the reproducible Student Activity on page 15.

One Fine Night

Write the word that makes the sentence tell about the picture.

1. It is _____.

        fall   **fan**   **for**

2. Kim and her dad are at the

  _____.

    make   **mall**   **man**

3. They go down a big _____.

                pal   **have**   **hall**

4. "Look over this _____, Kim."

           will   **wall**   **wax**

5. Kim is not _____.

         tall   **that**   **tap**

6. "Look at _____ the cats!"

        are   **and**   **all**

7. "Can I have the one with the _____?"

                 ban   **bat**   **ball**

8. "We will _____ Mom."

    come   **call**   **can**

Introducing Vocabulary

Apply word identification strategies.

IDENTIFY VOCABULARY WORDS Write the vocabulary words on the board and ask volunteers to identify any they know. Then read each word aloud and have children say them after you. Repeat the procedure several times. Remind children that they can use their knowledge of the sounds letters stand for and the clues you give them to recognize words. Give them the following clues and have a volunteer say and frame the word that answers each one: you can use this word to tell why (*because*); this is someone who might help you (*friend*); you find flowing water in this (*river*); how you might feel if you broke something by accident (*sorry*); a place where a family lives (*home*); the opposite of *lost* (*found*).

VOCABULARY DEFINED
because for the reason that
found discovered; past tense of *find*
friend a person you know well and like
home the place where someone lives
river a large stream of water
sorry feeling bad about something you did

Check understanding.

Ask children to write the vocabulary words on a of sheet of paper. Then ask the following questions. After children name the correct word, they should circle it on their papers.

- **Who can you tell a secret to?** *(friend)*
- **What word do you use to apologize?** *(sorry)*
- **If someone asks you "Why?", how might you begin your answer?** *(because)*
- **What word means "a big stream"?** *(river)*
- **Where do people live?** *(home)*
- **What word means "discovered"?** *(found)*

Children may be unfamiliar with some of the words in the title of the selection they are about to read. After distributing the vocabulary page, point to the title, "One Fine Night," read it aloud, and have children read it with you.

REPRODUCIBLE STUDENT ACTIVITY PAGE

INDEPENDENT PRACTICE See the reproducible Student Activity on page 17.

NOTE: The following vocabulary words from "Days With Frog and Toad" are reinforced in "One Fine Night." If children are unfamiliar with these words, point them out as you encounter them during reading: *alone, reason* (p. 22); *meadow* (p. 24); *spoiled, cheer* (p. 26); and *fine* (p. 29).

Name _____

One Fine Night

Read the story.

Choose from the underlined words above to complete each sentence.

1. Hal was sad _____ he was alone.

2. Hal _____ some _____ to call.

3. One was napping at _____.

4. The other said he was _____, but he was in

the _____.

Harcourt

Directed Reading

Pages 22–23 Point out each word in the title of the story and read it aloud with children. Then have them look at the illustration on page 22. Explain that Hal is the owl, and that he is sad because he is at home by himself.

Tell children to read pages 22–23 to find out what Hal does about being home alone. **What does Hal do about being alone?** (*He calls Rip.*) LITERAL: MAIN IDEA Model the thinking: **Hal wants Rip to come over, but Rip says he is napping.**

Pages 24–25 Ask children to look at the pictures on pages 24 and 25 and predict what will happen on these pages. Then have them read the pages to see if their predictions are correct. You might read aloud the word *meadow* on page 24 and explain its meaning. Then model the thinking: **On these two pages, Hal calls two more friends, Mack and Gil. He asks them to come over, but they are busy. Hal must feel very sad when none of his friends come over.**

Page 26 Ask a volunteer to read aloud the first two sentences on page 26. Help children read the words *spoiled* and *cheer*. Ask if children think Rip will be angry at Hal for spoiling his nap. Have them read on to find out. **Is Rip angry because Hal spoiled his nap?** (*no*) **How can you tell?** (Possible response: *He says he will call Hal back and cheer him up.*) INFERENTIAL: DETERMINE CHARACTERS' FEELINGS Have children read the rest of page 26 and discuss what Mack decides to do. Point out that Mack decides to find Hal.

Page 27 Ask children what they think Gil will decide to do next. Have them read page 27 to find out. Model the thinking: **Gil decides to call Hal. I can see that Hal's friends want him to be happy.**

Pages 28–29. Have children identify characters in the illustration on page 28. Ask what they are doing. Have children read page 29 to find out how the story ends. Use the illustration to model the thinking: **In the picture, I can see that the characters are all together now. Hal must be very happy because his friends are with him.** Discuss with children whether they agree with what the author writes on page 29.

SUMMARIZING THE SELECTION Ask children to think about what happened first, next, and last in "One Fine Night." Then have them summarize the story in three or four sentences. (Possible response: *Hal is lonely, so he calls some friends. At first, they are all busy and cannot come over. Then they decide to call Hal. They all go sailing together.*)

Answers to Think About It Questions

Page 29
1. They didn't want Hal to be sad and lonely. SUMMARY
2. Hal liked playing with friends more than playing alone. INTERPRETATION
3. Accept reasonable responses. TASK

Name _____

One Fine Night

Fill in the story map to tell about "One Fine Night." Use the words in the boxes.

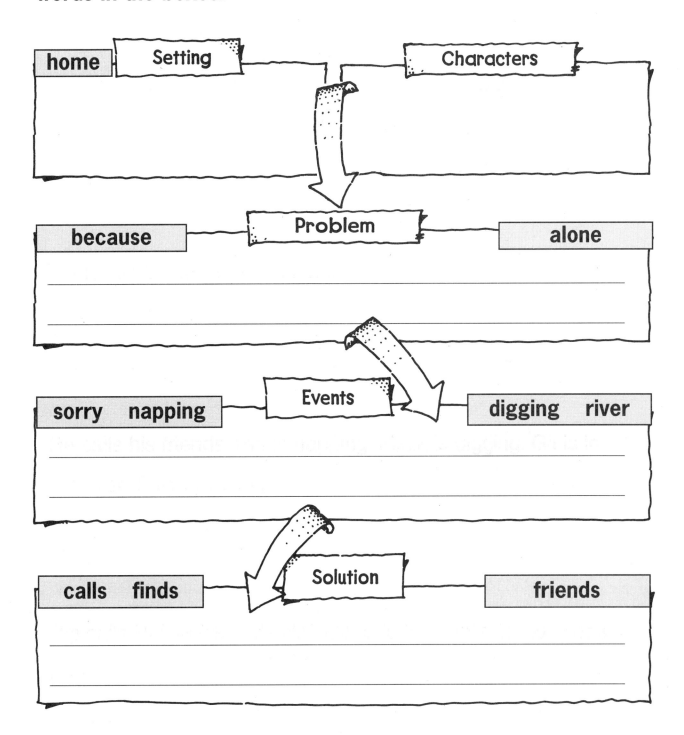

home | Setting | Characters

because | Problem | alone

sorry napping | Events | digging river

calls finds | Solution | friends

phonics

Just You and Me

by Bill E. Neder   **Use with *Blue Skies*, pages 30–37.**

Preteaching Skills: Short Vowel /o/o

Teach/Model

IDENTIFY THE SOUND Ask children to repeat the following sentence aloud several times: *This pot has a hot top.* Have children identify the words that have the /o/ sound. (*pot, hot, top*) Ask children to raise their hands each time they hear a word with the /o/ sound: *top, tip, tap, cap, pop, job, hot, hit.*

ASSOCIATE LETTERS TO THEIR SOUNDS Write the sentence *This pot has a hot top* on the board. Ask a volunteer to underline the words with the /o/ sound. (*pot, hot, top*) Tell children that in these words, the letter o stands for the /o/ sound. Have children read the underlined words with you. Then remind children that when a word has a vowel in between two consonants, the word usually has a short vowel sound. Ask children to identify the CVC pattern in *pot, hot,* and *top.*

WORD BLENDING Model reading the word *pot* by blending the sounds the letters stand for: Slide your hand under the letters and slowly elongate the sounds /ppoott/. Then read the word naturally and have volunteers repeat it. Have children take turns blending the sounds in each remaining word and reading them aloud.

Practice/Apply

APPLY THE SKILL *Vowel Substitution* Write the following words on the board, one at a time, and have children read them aloud. Then change the vowel in each one to form the word in parentheses. Have children take turns reading each new word.

pat (pot)   pit (pot)   hat (hot)   tap (top)   hip (hop)   map (mop)

Help children restate the generalization about the CVC pattern: When a vowel is between two consonants, the word usually has a short vowel sound.

DICTATION AND WRITING Have children number a sheet of paper 1–7. Dictate the following words, and have children write them. After each word is written, write it on the board so children can proofread their work. On their papers, they should draw a line through a misspelled word and write the correct spelling below it.

1. hot*   2. top   3. nod   4. pit   *Word appears in
5. mop*   6. map   7. not*   "Just You and Me."

Then dictate the following sentence: *The top on that pot is hot.*

READ LONGER WORDS *Compound Words* Write the word *myself* on the board. Tell children that when they see a longer word, they should look for smaller words they know inside it. Cover the word *self* and have children read the remaining word *my.* Then cover the word *my* and have children read the remaining word *self.* Finally, draw your hand under the entire word as children read it. Explain that a word made up of two smaller words is called a **compound word.** Then write the word *bobcat* on the board. Ask a volunteer to read the word aloud and explain how they were able to figure it out.

REPRODUCIBLE STUDENT ACTIVITY PAGE

INDEPENDENT PRACTICE See the reproducible Student Activity on page 21.

20   Grade 2 • Intervention Reader Teacher's Guide

Just You and Me

Read the story. Circle all the short *o* words.

Mom has a pot. Bob has the top.

Bob fills the pot. Mom makes it hot.

Bob got a mop. Mom looks in the pot.

Mom makes lots of jam. Bob is not sad!

Circle the word to complete each sentence. Write it on the line.

1. Mom got the _____.

       pit   pot   pat

2. Bob got a _____ for the pot.

    tap   tip   top

3. Mom made the pot _____.

    hit   hat   hot

4. Bob had to get the _____.

    mop   man   mad

5. Bob likes jam a _____!

    lid   lap   lot

Harcourt

Introducing Vocabulary

Apply word identification strategies.

IDENTIFY VOCABULARY WORDS Write the vocabulary words on the board and ask children to identify any they know. Then read the words aloud and have children say them after you. Repeat the procedure several times. Have children use their knowledge of the sounds that letters stand for and the clues you give them to recognize the words. Give them the following clues and have a volunteer say and frame the word that answers each one:

- **what you did when your favorite TV show was on** (*watched*)
- **what is in the classroom** (*desk*)
- **something white that falls in the winter** (*snow*)
- **made a noise like a tiger** (*roared*)
- **a place where teachers work** (*school*)
- **what you did when you took part in a game** (*played*)

VOCABULARY DEFINED
desk a piece of furniture with a flat top, used for writing
played took part in a game
roared made a loud, deep noise; laughed very hard
school a place for teaching and learning
snow water vapor that is frozen and falls from the sky in soft, white flakes
watched looked at carefully

Check understanding.

Ask children to write the vocabulary words on a sheet of paper. Then ask the following questions. After children name the correct word, they should circle that word on their papers.

> **Which word . . .**
> - **means "looked carefully at something"?** (*watched*)
> - **names a place where children go to learn?** (*school*)
> - **means "made a loud sound"?** (*roared*)
> - **tells what you did if you took part in a game?** (*played*)
> - **names something you see in winter?** (*snow*)
> - **names something you can put your books on?** (*desk*)

Children may be unfamiliar with some of the words in the title of the selection they are about to read. After distributing the vocabulary page, point to the title, "Just You and Me," read it aloud, and have children read it with you.

REPRODUCIBLE STUDENT ACTIVITY PAGE

INDEPENDENT PRACTICE See the reproducible Student Activity on page 23.

NOTE: The following vocabulary words from "Wilson Sat Alone" are reinforced in "Just You and Me." If children are unfamiliar with these words, point them out as you encounter them during reading: *clustered, groups* (p. 30); *gathered* (p. 31); *wandered* and *raced* (p. 33).

Just You and Me

Read the story.

Matt had no friends at <u>school.</u>

The friends <u>played,</u> but Matt sat at his <u>desk.</u>

"I will make a friend," he said.

Matt's friend <u>watched</u> him play.

Then the kids <u>roared,</u> "Will you come and play?"

Now the <u>snow</u> is gone, but Matt has lots of friends!

Write an underlined word to complete each sentence.

1. Matt had no friends at _____.

2. The friends _____, but Matt did not.

3. He sat at his _____ alone.

4. Matt made a friend out of _____.

5. Matt's snow friend _____ him play.

6. The kids _____ at Matt.

Directed Reading

Pages 30–31   Read aloud the title with children. Ask them to describe what they see in the picture on page 31. Explain that the boy who is sitting by himself feels sad. Ask children why he might be feeling sad. Then ask children to read page 30 to find out why the boy feels sad. You might point out and explain the meaning of the word *clustered*. **Why is the boy sad?** (Possible response: *because he has no friends at school*) INFERENTIAL: CAUSE AND EFFECT   **What do the boy's parents tell him to do?** (Possible response: *to make some friends at school*) LITERAL: NOTE DETAILS   Model the thinking: **I see that the boy listens to his parents and makes a snow friend.**

Page 31   Ask children to describe the picture on page 31. Then have them read the page. You might point out and explain the word *gathered*. **How did the boy make Bob?** (Possible response: *He rolled three balls of snow, stacked them, got a pot for a hat, and got a mop for him to hold.*) INFERENTIAL: SEQUENCE   **Do you think a snowman would make a good friend? Why or why not?** (Responses will vary.) CRITICAL: MAKE JUDGMENTS

Page 32   Ask children to describe what is happening in the picture on page 32. Then have children read page 32 to find out what kind of friend Bob is. Model the thinking: **Bob seems to be a good friend for the boy. The boy says that Bob watches everything he does. Do you think that Bob is really watching the boy? Why or why not?** (Possible response: *No. A snowman is made of snow, and it can't really watch or play.*) CRITICAL: REALITY AND FANTASY

Page 33   Ask children what they think will happen now that the other kids have noticed Bob. Have them read page 33 to find out. You might point out and explain the words *wandered* and *raced* aloud before children begin reading. **What happens when the kids see Bob?** (Possible response: *They come over to see him.*) LITERAL: NOTE DETAILS   **What do you think will happen next?** (Responses will vary.) CRITICAL: MAKE PREDICTIONS

Page 34   Ask children to read page 34. **Is this what you thought would happen?** (Responses will vary.) CRITICAL: CONFIRM PREDICTIONS

Page 35   Have children view the illustration and read page 35. Ask them to tell what is different about the setting of the story and what is different about the boy. (Possible responses: *It is hot now; there is no more snow; the boy is not sad anymore because he has friends.*) **What happened to Bob?** (Possible response: *He melted.*) INFERENTIAL: CAUSE AND EFFECT   Discuss with children how Bob helped the boy make friends.

SUMMARIZING THE SELECTION   Have children summarize the selection by telling what happened at the beginning, middle, and end of the story in three or four sentences.

Answers to Think About It Questions

Page 36
1. The boy makes a friend out of snow. SUMMARY
2. Bob can't be there because he is made of snow. He melts when it is hot. INTERPRETATION
3. Accept reasonable responses. TASK

Page 37   For instruction on the Focus Skill: Characters' Feelings and Actions, see page 37 in *Blue Skies*.

Name _____

Just You and Me

Write *beginning*, *middle*, or *end* to show when each thing happened.

_____   _____   _____

Now write what happened in the story. Use the words in the boxes in your answers.

Beginning:	school played friends

Middle:	snow loved Bob roared

End:	friends desk

Harcourt

Phonics

Turtle Makes a Wish

by Anne W. Phillips **Use with *Blue Skies*, pages 38–45.**

Preteaching Skills: Blends with *s, r, l*

Teach/Model

IDENTIFY THE SOUND Read the following sentence aloud and have children repeat it three times: *Stan can skip and snap.* Ask children to identify the words that begin with the /s/ sound combined with another consonant sound. (*Stan, skip, snap*)

ASSOCIATE LETTERS TO THEIR SOUNDS Write on the board the sentence *Stan can skip and snap.* Underline the consonant blends in *Stan, skip,* and *snap.* Tell children that when they see two consonants blended together in a word, they should try blending together the sounds of the two letters. Model blending two consonant sounds: Slide your hand under the letters *St* in *Stan* as you slowly elongate the sounds /ssttaann/. Then read the word *Stan* naturally and have children repeat it. Repeat the process with the words *skip* and *snap.* Then write these words on the board: *stop, trip, drag, clip,* and *flag.* Have volunteers take turns blending the sounds in each word and reading them aloud.

Practice/Apply

APPLY THE SKILL *Consonant Substitution* Write on the board the first word in each pair of the following words, one at a time, and have children read them aloud. Make the changes necessary to form the words in parentheses. Have children take turns reading aloud each new word.

pin (spin)	skip (slip)	prop (drop)	band (brand)	sill (still)
top (stop)	grip (trip)	grab (crab)	dip (drip)	sand (grand)

DICTATION AND WRITING Have children number a sheet of paper 1–8. Dictate the following words, and have children write them. After each word is written, write it on the board so children can proofread their work. On their papers, they should draw a line through a misspelled word and write the correct spelling below it.

1. snap*	2. skid	3. stop	4. grab	*Word appears in "Turtle Makes a Wish."*
5. frog*	6. drop	7. still*	8. small	

Then dictate the following sentence: *Dan skids to a stop.*

READ LONGER WORDS *Ending: -ing; Double Consonants* Write the word *clapping* on the board. Remind children that when they come to a longer word, they should try looking for a shorter word they know inside it. Cover *ping* and ask children to read the remaining word. Model blending the word parts *clap* and *ping* to say the whole word. Then have children do the same. Follow the same procedure with the words *skipping, swimming,* and *snapping.*

REPRODUCIBLE STUDENT ACTIVITY PAGE

INDEPENDENT PRACTICE See the reproducible Student Activity on page 27.

Turtle Makes a Wish

Read the story. Circle all the words that begin with two consonants.

Stan has a cat and a flag. Fran has a hat. Stan and Fran skip.

Stan trips. He drops his cat and his flag. Fran has a plan.

Fran grabs her hat. Fran grabs the cat. Fran grabs the flag.

Stan is glad. His cat is glad. Stan and the cat like Fran.

Write the word that best completes each sentence.

1. Stan has a cat and a _____.

flag   skip   plan

2. _____ has a hat.

Cat   Fran   Stan

3. Stan _____ the flag.

skips   plans   drops

4. Fran _____ the cat and the flag.

grabs   skips   drops

5. Stan and the cat are _____.

clams   small   glad

Harcourt

Introducing Vocabulary

Apply word identification strategies.

IDENTIFY VOCABULARY WORDS Write the vocabulary words on the board, and ask children to identify any they know. Then read each word aloud and have children say each one after you. Repeat the procedure several times. Have children use their knowledge of the sounds that letters stand for and the clues you give them to recognize the words. Give children the following clues and have a volunteer say and frame the word that answers each one:

- **a place where people can see elephants and tigers** (*zoo*)
- **what elephants and tigers are** (*animals*)
- **how animals feel when they need food** (*hungry*)
- **a word you could use to talk about yourself** (*myself*)
- **what you might do if you want something** (*wish*)
- **If you got what you wished for, you could say that your wish came ____.** (*true*)

Check understanding.

Have children write the vocabulary words on a sheet of paper. Then ask the following questions. After children name the correct word, they should circle that word on their papers.

- **What word is another way to say *me*?** (*myself*)
- **What word tells what a cow and a dog are?** (*animals*)
- **Where might you go to see animals that come from faraway places?** (*zoo*)
- **What word means "to want something you don't have"?** (*wish*)
- **Which word could you use to tell about something that really happened?** (*true*)
- **How do people usually feel if they haven't eaten for a while?** (*hungry*)

Children may be unfamiliar with some of the words in the title of the selection they are about to read. After distributing the vocabulary page, point to the title, "Turtle Makes a Wish," read it aloud, and have children read it with you.

VOCABULARY DEFINED
animals living creatures, such as dogs, horses, and fish
hungry feeling the need for food
myself me
true really happened
wish to want something you don't have
zoo a place where people can go to see animals

REPRODUCIBLE STUDENT ACTIVITY PAGE

INDEPENDENT PRACTICE See the reproducible Student Activity on page 29.

NOTE: The following vocabulary words from "The Mixed-Up Chameleon" are reinforced in "Turtle Makes a Wish." If children are unfamiliar with these words, point them out as you encounter them during reading: *dull, handsome, hardly* (p. 38); *spotted* (p. 39); *sideways, exciting* (p. 40); and *sparkling* (p. 41).

Turtle Makes a Wish

Read the story. Then write an answer to each question in the web. Use the underlined words in your answers.

Turtle was on a log in the river. When he was <u>hungry</u>, he got a snack. When he was hot, he swam. But Turtle was sad.

"I do not like <u>myself</u>," he said. "I am small. I <u>wish</u> I was tall." Turtle liked to wish.

Turtle went to the <u>zoo</u>. He saw tall <u>animals</u>. What did Turtle wish? Will his wish come <u>true</u>? Read "Turtle Makes a Wish" to find out.

What did Turtle do when he was hot?
_____
_____

When did Turtle get a snack?
_____
_____

Why was Turtle sad?
_____
_____

Turtle

Where did Turtle go?
_____
_____

What did Turtle see there?
_____
_____

Harcourt

Directed Reading

Page 38

Have children look at the illustration and name the animals they see. *(turtle, frog, fish)* Ask: **Do you think Turtle is happy or sad? How do you know?** (Possible response: *Sad. His face looks sad.*) METACOGNITIVE: DRAW CONCLUSIONS Have children read the page to find out why Turtle is sad. Point out and read aloud the words *dull, handsome,* and *hardly.* You might explain that the word *dull* means "not bright or shiny." Model the thinking: **Turtle is sad because he is small and dull. He doesn't like himself.**

Page 39

Have children look at the picture on page 39. **Where is Turtle now?** *(at a zoo)* LITERAL: NOTE DETAILS Have children read page 39 to find out what Turtle does next. Model the thinking: **Turtle sees a giraffe. He wishes he was tall like the giraffe. What do you think will happen next?** (Answers will vary.) INFERENTIAL: MAKE PREDICTIONS

Page 40

Have children read page 40 to confirm their predictions. You might help children decode the words *sideways* and *exciting* and discuss their meanings. Then model the thinking: **Turtle's wish came true. He has grown very tall. Is Turtle happy now? How can you tell?** (Possible response: *No. Turtle says he is still not handsome.*) INFERENTIAL: DETERMINE CHARACTERS' EMOTIONS

Page 41

Discuss with children whether they think Turtle will ever be happy with the way he looks. Then have children read page 41 aloud. **What does Turtle wish next?** *(that he could be handsome)* LITERAL: IDENTIFY CHARACTERS' EMOTIONS Point to the illustration and say: **I see that Turtle's wish comes true. His shell is covered with bird feathers.** Help children read the word *sparkling* and explain its meaning. **Do you think Turtle is happy now? Why or why not?** *(Yes. He seems happy and he is not dull anymore.)* LITERAL: IDENTIFY CHARACTERS' EMOTIONS

Page 42

Before they read page 42, ask children to predict what will happen when Turtle gets home. Then have them read page 42 silently to find out what the river animals say when they see Turtle. Model the thinking: **The animals don't seem to know Turtle. He can't swim like a turtle anymore.**

Page 43

Have children read page 43. **How does Turtle feel now? Why?** *(He is sad because he wants to be himself.)* INFERENTIAL: DETERMINE CHARACTERS' EMOTIONS Ask children to read page 43 to find out what Turtle will wish for next, and say: **Turtle makes another wish. This time he wishes he could be himself. Do you think his wish will come true?** (Responses will vary.) INFERENTIAL: MAKE PREDICTIONS

Page 44

Have children look at the illustration and read the text on page 44 to confirm their predictions. **How do you think Frog and Fish feel about having Turtle back?** *(They are glad to see him.)* INFERENTIAL: IDENTIFY CHARACTERS' EMOTIONS Discuss with children what Turtle learned—that it is best to be yourself.

SUMMARIZING THE SELECTION Ask children to say four sentences that tell the most important events in the story.

Answers to Think About It Questions

Page 45

1. They miss the real Turtle, who can swim in the river and snap up ants. SUMMARY
2. He found out that it is best to be himself. INTERPRETATION
3. Accept reasonable responses. TASK

Name _____

Turtle Makes a Wish

Complete the flowchart with words from the box to tell what happens in "Turtle Makes a Wish."

myself	zoo	animals	true	wish	hungry

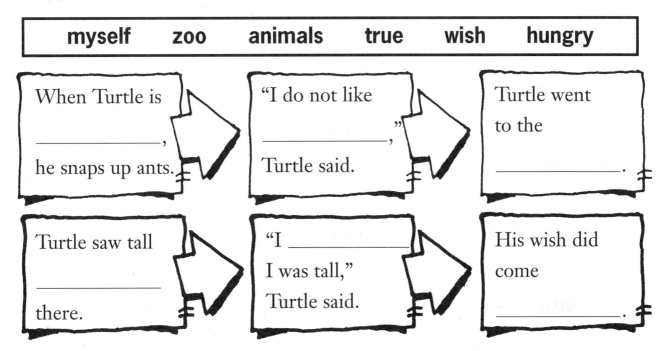

When Turtle is _____, he snaps up ants.

"I do not like _____," Turtle said.

Turtle went to the _____.

Turtle saw tall _____ there.

"I _____ I was tall," Turtle said.

His wish did come _____.

Write the answers to these questions to tell the rest of the story.

1. What did Turtle wish for next? _____

_____

2. What did the animals in the river ask Turtle when he got home?

_____

3. What did Turtle wish for at the end of the story? _____

_____

4. What did you like best in this story? _____

_____

A Turnip's Tale

by Lois Bick   **Use with *Blue Skies*, pages 46–53.**

Preteaching Skills: Short Vowel /e/e

Teach/Model

IDENTIFY THE SOUND Ask children to repeat the following sentence aloud several times: *Jen will pet the red hen.* Have children identify the words in the sentence that have the /e/ sound. *(Jen, pet, red, hen)* Ask children to raise their hands each time they hear a word with the /e/ sound in these words: *stop, step, men, bet, cap, mat, met.*

ASSOCIATE LETTERS TO THEIR SOUNDS Write the sentence *Jen will pet the red hen* on the board and have a volunteer underline the words that contain the letter *e.* Tell children that in these words, the letter *e* stands for the /e/ sound. Have children read the underlined words with you. Then remind children that when a word has a vowel in between two consonants, the vowel sound is usually short. Ask children to identify the CVC pattern in *Jen, pet, red,* and *hen.*

WORD BLENDING Model reading the word *Jen* by blending the sounds the letters stand for: Slide your hand under the letters as you slowly elongate the sounds /jjeenn/. Then read the word *Jen* naturally. Have children do the same. Then model replacing initial consonants to form new /e/ words such as those below. Have children take turns blending the sounds to read each new word aloud.

Jen (men, ten)   pet (let, get)   red (bed, led)

Practice/Apply

APPLY THE SKILL *Vowel Substitution* Write the first word in each pair below on the board and have children read them aloud. Then make the changes necessary to form the word in parentheses. Have volunteers take turns reading each new word.

pan (pen)	big (beg)	rod (red)	stop (step)
tin (ten)	man (men)	mat (met)	sit (set)

DICTATION AND WRITING Have children number a sheet of paper 1–8. Dictate the following words, and have children write them. After each word is written, write it on the board so children can proofread their work. They should draw a line through a misspelled word and write the correct spelling below it.

1. men*	2. set	3. yes	4. get*
5. bed	6. well*	7. nest	8. best*

*Word appears in "A Turnip's Tale."

Then dictate the following sentence: *Ted let the hen in the pen.*

READ LONGER WORDS *Endings -ed, -es; Ending -le; Break Between Double Consonants* Write the words *dress* and *dresses* on the board. Remind children that they can look for words they know in longer words. Cover the *-es* in *dresses* with your hand, and ask a volunteer to read *dress* aloud. Then uncover the *-es* ending and read aloud the word *dresses*, asking children to repeat it. Then ask children to read the following words aloud and explain how they figured them out: *presses, helped, messes, stopped.* Next, write the word *settle* on the board. Ask which part of the word says /set/ and which part says /təl/. Then ask what /set/ and /təl/ together say. Repeat the procedure with *riddle* and *kettle.*

REPRODUCIBLE STUDENT ACTIVITY PAGE

....

INDEPENDENT PRACTICE See the reproducible Student Activity on page 33.

Name _____

A Turnip's Tale

Write the word that best completes each sentence.

wet	nest	bell	ten	bed	sled	men

1. Two _____ go to the zoo.

2. The cat is on the _____ .

3. Can you see the _____ ?

4. Her _____ can go down.

5. The _____ is in the tree.

6. These animals are _____ .

7. There are _____ red apples.

Harcourt

Introducing Vocabulary

Apply word identification strategies.

IDENTIFY VOCABULARY WORDS Display the vocabulary words on the board and ask children to identify any they know. Then read each word aloud and have children say them after you. Repeat the procedure several times. Have children use their knowledge of the sounds that letters stand for and the clues you give them to recognize the words. Give them the following clues and have a volunteer say and frame the word that answers each one:

- **what you did when you opened the refrigerator door** *(pulled)*
- **a small animal that hides from cats** *(mouse)*
- **means "was able to"** *(could)*
- **said something in a loud voice** *(called)*
- **a mother or grandmother** *(woman)*
- **means "another time"** *(again)*

VOCABULARY DEFINED
again another time; once more
called said something, often in a loud voice
could was able to
mouse a small animal with fur, a pointed nose, and a long tail
pulled used force to move something toward you
woman an adult female person

Check understanding.

Ask children to write the vocabulary words on a piece of paper. Then ask the following questions. After children name the correct word, have them circle that word on their papers.

> **Which word . . .**
> - **means "moved something toward you"?** *(pulled)*
> - **names a person?** *(woman)*
> - **makes sense in this sentence: I wish I ___ go with you.** *(could)*
> - **names a small animal?** *(mouse)*
> - **tells about doing something over and over?** *(again)*
> - **names what you did when you yelled to a friend?** *(called)*

Children may be unfamiliar with some of the words in the title of the selection they are about to read. After distributing the vocabulary page, point to the title, "A Turnip's Tale," read it aloud, and have children read it with you.

REPRODUCIBLE STUDENT ACTIVITY PAGE

INDEPENDENT PRACTICE See the reproducible Student Activity on page 35.

NOTE: The following vocabulary words from "The Enormous Turnip" are reinforced in "A Turnip's Tale." If children are unfamiliar with these words, point them out as you encounter them during reading: *planted, turnip, grew, enormous* (p. 46); *granddaughter* (p. 49); and *strong* (p. 50).

Name _____

A Turnip's Tale

Look at the pictures. Then write a word from the box to complete each sentence below.

again	called	could	mouse	pulled	woman

1. A _____ had a turnip that fell into a well.

2. She _____ for help.

3. They all _____ the turnip.

4. They _____ not get it out.

5. Then they pulled the turnip _____ .

6. Can a small _____ help them? Find out when you read "A Turnip's Tale."

Harcourt

Directed Reading

Page 46

Read the title aloud with children. Explain, if necessary, that a turnip is a rounded white-and-purple root vegetable that grows underground. Ask a volunteer to describe the illustration. Then have children read page 46. Ask: **What do you think will happen to the turnip?** (Responses will vary.) CRITICAL: MAKE PREDICTIONS

Page 47

Have children look at the picture on page 47 and read the text. **What has happened to the turnip?** *(It has fallen into a well.)* LITERAL: NOTE DETAILS Make sure children understand that a well stores water, and that its water level goes up and down. Tell children: **The woman is upset. She wants to get the turnip out of the well. What do you think she will do next?** (Responses will vary.) CRITICAL: MAKE PREDICTIONS

Page 48

Ask children to look at the pictures on pages 48 and 49. If necessary, explain that the bucket at the bottom of the well is used to pull water from the well. Then have children read page 48 to find out what the woman does to try to get the turnip out. Say: **I read that the woman pulled and pulled. Then she called for help.**

Page 49

Ask children to read page 49. **Who was the first person to help the woman?** *(the woman's granddaughter)* LITERAL: SEQUENCE **Then who came to help?** *(some men)* LITERAL: SEQUENCE **Who do you think will come to help next?** (Responses will vary.) CRITICAL: MAKE PREDICTIONS

Page 50

Have children read page 50 to learn what happens next. **Who is helping now?** *(a mouse)* LITERAL: NOTE DETAILS **How does the woman feel about the mouse?** (Possible response: *She doesn't think he is strong. She thinks he is a little pest.*) INFERENTIAL: DETERMINE CHARACTERS' EMOTIONS Tell children: **The mouse shows the others how to fill the well with water to bring up the turnip. Do you think the mouse's plan will work?** (Responses will vary.) CRITICAL: MAKE PREDICTIONS

Page 51

Have children look at the picture to confirm their predictions. Then have children read page 51 to find out how the characters feel now. **How do the people feel about what has happened?** *(They are all very glad.)* LITERAL: IDENTIFY CHARACTERS' EMOTIONS Model the thinking: **Think about what the woman learned from the mouse. She learned that help can come from unexpected places. The people tried to use strength to pull up the turnip, but the mouse used brain power.**

SUMMARIZING THE SELECTION Ask children to reread the story and then create a short comic strip that tells the most important events. Encourage children to write or dictate a caption for each drawing. (Possible captions: *A turnip fell into the well. The woman could not pull it out. She called for help. The girl, the men, and the mouse all helped get it out.*) INFERENTIAL: SUMMARIZE

Answers to Think About It Questions

Page 52

1. The mouse and the others add water to make the turnip come up to the top. SUMMARY
2. She said that the mouse was little and not strong. INTERPRETATION
3. Accept reasonable responses. TASK

Page 53

For instruction on the Focus Skill: Sequence, see page 53 in *Blue Skies*.

A Turnip's Tale

These events are from "A Turnip's Tale." They are out of order. Write a number in front of each one to show the right order.

_____ A mouse came to help.

_____ The granddaughter asked some men to help.

_____ The turnip fell into a well.

_____ They all pulled and pulled, but they could not get the turnip out.

_____ The woman called her granddaughter.

Now finish the story. Write what happened on the lines below.

_____

_____

_____

_____

_____

_____

_____

_____

_____

Tools That Help

by Beverly A. Dietz   **Use with *Blue Skies*, pages 54–61.**

Preteaching Skills: Digraph /sh/*sh*

Teach/Model

IDENTIFY THE SOUND Have children repeat the following sentence aloud three times: *She sells shells by the shore.* Ask children to name the words that have the /sh/ sound. (*she, shells, shore*)

ASSOCIATE LETTERS TO THEIR SOUNDS Write the sentence *She sells shells by the shore* on the board, and ask a volunteer to underline the letters *sh* where they appear. Tell children that when the letters *s* and *h* come together, they usually stand for one sound—the /sh/ sound in *she, shells,* and *shore.* Now write the words below on the board. Have volunteers take turns reading the first four words aloud.

ship, fish, shop, mash, wish, cash, dish, rash, swish, trash, smash

WORD BLENDING Model blending the sounds the letters stand for in the word *ship*: Slide your hand under the *sh* and slowly elongate the sounds /shiipp/. Then say the word *ship* naturally and have children do the same. Point out the last three letters in *fish* and *mash.* Tell children that if they can read *fish* and *mash,* they can read words that rhyme with *fish* and *mash.* Point to the remaining seven words on the board, one at a time, and have children take turns reading aloud each new word.

Practice/Apply

APPLY THE SKILL *Consonant Substitution* Write on the board the first word in each pair, omitting the underlines, and have children read them aloud. Then substitute each underlined consonant with the letters *sh* to form the words in parentheses. Have children take turns reading the new words aloud.

b<u>ed</u> (shed)	<u>p</u>op (shop)	ca<u>b</u> (cash)	a<u>s</u> (ash)
<u>b</u>in (shin)	<u>h</u>ip (ship)	wi<u>n</u> (wish)	ra<u>n</u> (rash)

DICTATION AND WRITING Have children number a sheet of paper 1–7. Dictate the following words, and have children write them. After each word is written, display it so children can proofread their work. They should draw a line through a mis-spelled word and write the correct spelling below it.

1. shop	2. shed	3. ship	4. shin
5. cash	6. wish*	7. dishes*	

Word appears in "Tools That Help."

Dictate the following sentence for children to write: *Set the trash can in the shed.*

READ LONGER WORDS *Two-Syllable Words with VCCV; Ending -es* Write the word *wishes* on the board. Remind children to look for word parts they know. Cover the *-es* ending and have children read the word *wish.* Then uncover the *-es* ending and have them read the whole word. Remind children that when they see the letters *sh* together, they stand for one sound. Have children apply what they have learned to read the words *dishes* and *flashes.*

REPRODUCIBLE STUDENT ACTIVITY PAGE

INDEPENDENT PRACTICE See the reproducible Student Activity on page 39.

Name _____

Tools That Help

Fill in the oval in front of the sentence that tells about the picture.

1 ◯ Ben hands her his cash.
◯ Ben makes a dash to the shed.
◯ Ben makes a wish.

2 ◯ Tad looks at the big ship.
◯ Tad has a pet fish.
◯ Tad has lost his dish.

3 ◯ Jen drops the dish.
◯ Jen sees a red fish.
◯ Jen is on a ship.

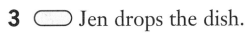

4 ◯ The shed fell over.
◯ I see a hen on the ship.
◯ The hen is in the shed.

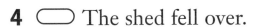

5 ◯ The cat has a fish.
◯ The cat sits by the shop.
◯ Now a cat is in the shack!

6 ◯ They wish they had a ball and bat.
◯ They find a shell.
◯ They make a fast dash.

Harcourt

Introducing Vocabulary

Apply word identification strategies.

LOOK FOR FAMILIAR SPELLING PATTERNS Write the vocabulary words on the board and ask children to try to read them silently. Remind children that they can sometimes figure out a new word by looking for spelling patterns they know. Point out the CVC spelling pattern in *jobs*. Call on volunteers to read this word aloud and tell how they were able to figure it out. (*When there is only one vowel in a word and it comes in between two consonants, it usually stands for a short vowel sound.*)

Have a volunteer cover the *ing* in *helping*. Point out the CVC spelling pattern in *help*, and have children read *help* and then *helping*. Model blending as needed. Have children use their knowledge of the sounds that the letters stand for and the clues you give them to recognize the remaining words. Give them the following clues and have volunteers say and frame the word that answers each one: a grown-up (*adult*); what you are doing in school (*learning*); got money for doing a job (*paid*); this is something you can do to earn money (*work*).

Check understanding.

Ask children to write the vocabulary words on a sheet of paper. Then ask the questions that follow. After children name the correct word, have them circle that word on their papers.

- **What is another word for a grown-up?** (*adult*)
- **What word means "tasks"?** (*jobs*)
- **What are students doing when they are taught something new?** (*learning*)
- **What might you get when you finish a job?** (*paid*)
- **Tom is drying the dishes after his dad washes them. What is Tom doing?** (*helping*)
- **What word tells what adults do at their jobs?** (*work*)

Children may be unfamiliar with some of the words in the title of the selection they are about to read. After distributing the vocabulary page, point to the title, "Tools That Help," read it aloud, and have children read it with you.

REPRODUCIBLE STUDENT ACTIVITY PAGE

INDEPENDENT PRACTICE See the reproducible Student Activity on page 41.

NOTE: The following vocabulary words from "Helping Out" are reinforced in "Tools That Help." If children are unfamiliar with these words, point them out as you encounter them during reading: *chores* (p. 54); *alongside, sprout* (p. 55); *simple, tool* (p. 56); and *engine* (p. 57).

Name ______________________

REPRODUCIBLE STUDENT ACTIVITY PAGE

Tools That Help

Read each sentence. Write the word from the box to complete each sentence.

adult	**helping**	**job**	**learning**	**paid**	**work**

1.

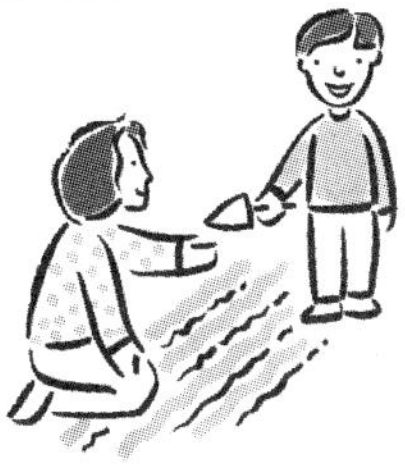

Ted is ______________________ his mom.

2.

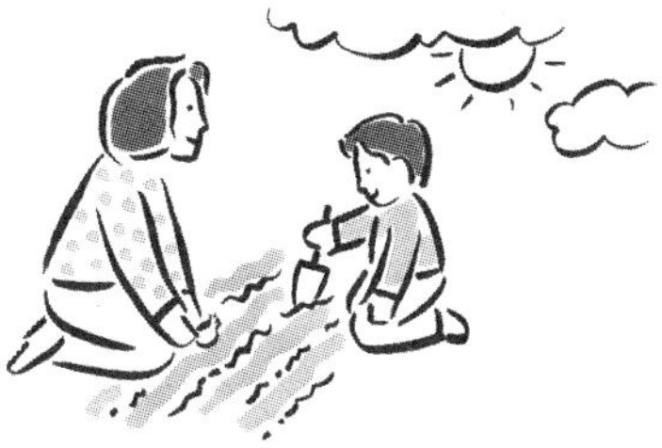

Ted and his mom like to ______________________.

3.

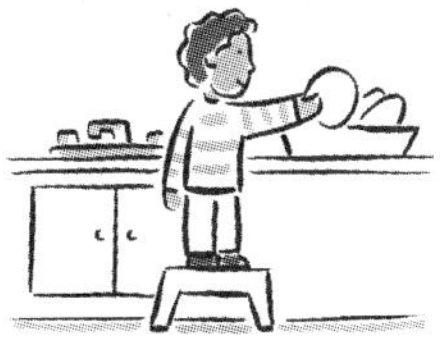

Jim's ______________________ is to do the dishes.

4.

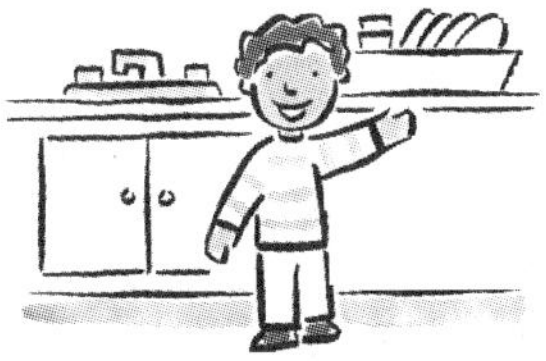

Jim does not get ______________ to do the dishes, but he likes to help out.

5.

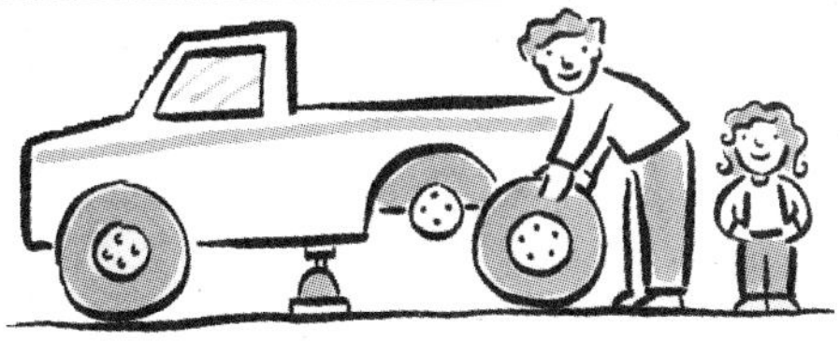

An ______________________ like Tish's dad has to fix this.

6.

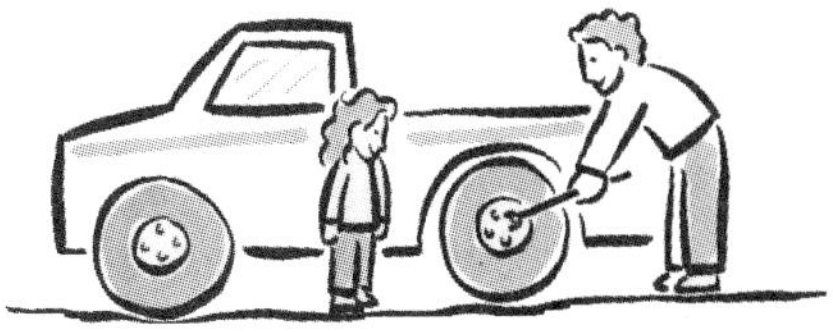

Tish is ______________________ how to help her dad with this big job.

Directed Reading

Pages 54–55   Read the title of the story aloud with children. Ask them to describe what they see in the picture. Explain that this selection is told by two children who interviewed other kids about the chores they do. Point out the word *chores* and, if necessary, explain that *chores* are jobs people do to help out at home.

Have children read pages 54–55 to learn what the kids in the story want to know and what they learned. If necessary, help children decode the story words *alongside* and *sprout* on page 55. **How does Ted help his mother?** (*He digs holes in the dirt with his tools.*) LITERAL: NOTE DETAILS

Page 56   Have children discuss the illustration on page 56. Then read the page aloud with children. Help them decode *simple* by blending the sounds in the two syllables, /sim/ and /pəl/. **Do you agree with Jim that washing dishes is a simple job? Why or why not?** (Possible response: *Yes, it is easy because you just need to make sure the dishes get clean with soap and warm water.*) CRITICAL: IDENTIFY WITH CHARACTERS

Page 57   Have children describe what is happening in the picture on page 57. Identify the car engine and the wrench. Tell children to read the page to find out how Tish helps her dad. You might point out the word *engine* in the text and read it aloud. **Why is fixing an engine a job for an adult and not for a kid?** (Possible responses: *It is too hard for kids to fix a car engine by themselves; you need to know the safety rules, the parts of the car, and how to use special tools.*) INFERENTIAL: GENERALIZE   Model the thinking: **Tish's dad needs her help, though. She gets tools for him to use. The kids in the story seem to be having fun helping out.**

Page 58   Have children summarize what they have learned so far about ways that kids can help out at home. Then have them look at the illustration on page 58 and discuss the job the boy has just finished. Then have them read page 58. **What work did Ben do?** (*He painted the fence.*) INFERENTIAL: DRAW CONCLUSIONS

Pages 59–60   Ask children to read page 59 to learn about Pat's chore.
What is Pat's chore? (*walking her dog, Shep*) LITERAL: NOTE DETAILS   Say: **Pat likes her chore because she says it is like playing.** Have children read page 60. Then discuss with them which of the chores they read about they would enjoy doing.

SUMMARIZING THE SELECTION Ask children to think about the chores they read about in "Tools That Help." Then have them summarize the story in three sentences by telling about the different ways children can help out at home.

Answers to Think About It Questions

Page 61
1. Possible response: The kids wash dishes, help fix an engine, and walk the dog.
   SUMMARY
2. Possible response: Pat walks the dog Shep, but you can also play with dogs during walks. INTERPRETATION
3. Accept reasonable responses. TASK

Name _____

Tools That Help

Complete the puzzle using words from the box.

| digging | learning | job | paid | helping | tools | chore |

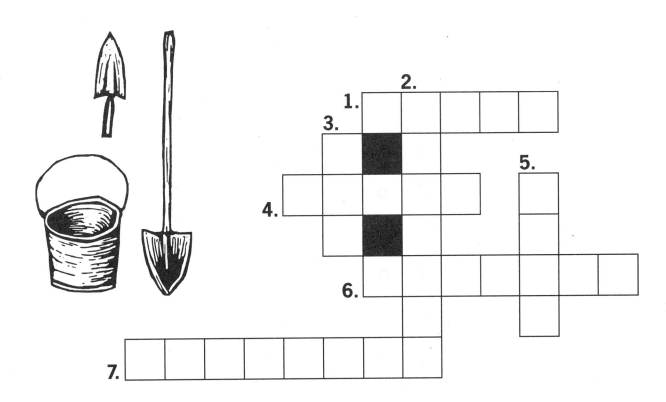

Across

1. Pat's _____ is walking her dog.

4. Some kids used _____ to help with the jobs.

6. Ted likes _____ with his mom.

7. Tish is _____ as she works.

Down

2. Jim likes _____ out at home.

3. Tish said that fixing an engine is a _____ for an adult.

5. Jim is not _____ for washing the dishes.

Harcourt

The Promise

by Susan McCloskey   **Use with _Blue Skies_, pages 62–69.**

Preteaching Skills: Short Vowel /u/u

Teach/Model

IDENTIFY THE SOUND Have children repeat the following sentence aloud several times: _A bug in the mud cannot run._ Ask children to identify the words in the sentence that have the /u/ sound. (_bug, mud, run_)

ASSOCIATE LETTERS TO THEIR SOUNDS Write this sentence on the board: _A bug in the mud cannot run._ Ask children to underline the words that contain the letter _u_. Tell children that in these words, the letter _u_ stands for the /u/ sound. Have children read the underlined words with you. Remind children that when a word has a vowel in between two or more consonants, the word usually has the short vowel sound.

WORD BLENDING Model reading the word _hug_ by blending the sounds the letters stand for: Slide your hand under the letters as you slowly elongate the sounds /hhuugg/. Then read the word naturally. Have children do the same. Then have children take turns blending the sounds in the following list of words and reading them aloud: _shut, cub, dug, cut, rub, snug, nut, stub._

Practice/Apply

APPLY THE SKILL _Vowel Substitution_ Write each of the following words on the board, and have children read it aloud. Then make the change necessary to form the word in parentheses. Ask children to take turns reading each new word aloud.

not (nut)   ham (hum)   bog (bug)   tag (tug)
mesh (mush)   rib (rub)   fan (fun)   bat (but)

DICTATION AND WRITING Have children number a sheet of paper 1–7. Dictate the following words, and have children write them. After each word is written, write it on the board so children can proofread their work. On their papers, they should draw a line through a misspelled word and write the correct spelling above it.

1. fun*   2. dug*   3. tub   4. plug   *Word appears in
5. jump*   6. hugged*   7. tugging*   "The Promise."

Then dictate the following sentence: _The bug had fun in the tub._

READ LONGER WORDS _Review Breaking Two-Syllable Words with a Double Consonant; Review Ending -ing_ Write the word _running_ on the board. Remind children that when they see a longer word, they should look for smaller words and word parts in it. Model the strategy with the word _running_. Point out the _-ing_ ending. Explain that when _-ing_ is added to _run_, the consonant _n_ is doubled. Then help children point out word bits and parts to read these words: _rushing, hugging, rubbing, cutting._ Next, ask volunteers to read the following words and explain how they were able to figure them out: _drumming, blushing, plugging, crushing._

REPRODUCIBLE STUDENT ACTIVITY PAGE

INDEPENDENT PRACTICE See the reproducible Student Activity on page 45.

The Promise

Read the sentences. Look at the picture. Then do what the sentences tell you.

1. Ned has a jug. Make it red.

2. Make a cup for Ned.

3. Find the plums. Make an apple to go with the plums.

4. Make the sun over the trees.

5. Make a red bug on a tree.

6. A pup runs to Ned. Make it black.

7. Find the animal that likes nuts. Make some nuts for it.

Now circle the words in the sentences that have the short *u* sound.

Harcourt

Introducing Vocabulary

Apply word identification strategies.

IDENTIFY VOCABULARY WORDS Display the vocabulary words, and ask children to identify words they know. Then remind children that knowing the sounds that letters stand for can help them read new words. Point to each vocabulary word and read it aloud. Have children read it aloud after you.

Check understanding.

Discuss the meaning of each vocabulary word with children. Then ask children to write the vocabulary words on a sheet of paper. Ask each of the following questions. Have children name the correct word and then circle it on their papers.

Which word . . .
- means "the opposite of *stop*"? *(start)*
- tells what birds do when they move through the air? *(fly)*
- tells what dolls, yo-yos, and tops are? *(toys)*
- means "used money at a store to get something"? *(bought)*
- names a machine that can travel through the air? *(plane)*

Children may be unfamiliar with a word in the title of the selection they will read. Distribute the vocabulary page. Then point to the title, "The Promise," read it aloud, and have children read it with you.

REPRODUCIBLE STUDENT ACTIVITY PAGE

INDEPENDENT PRACTICE See the reproducible Student Activity on page 47.

NOTE: The following vocabulary words from "Mr. Putter and Tabby Fly the Plane" are reinforced in "The Promise." If children are unfamiliar with these words, point them out as you encounter them during reading: *promise, directions* (p. 62); *crane* (p. 63); *twitched* (p. 64); and *worry* (p. 65).

The Promise

Read the ad.

Crump's Toy Shop
Big Sale Today!

Mr. Crump's Toy Shop has all the **toys** you need. If you have not **bought** a toy in a while, come in!

There are toys that **fly**. This **plane** is fun to play with. You can **start** it up and watch it go.

Mr. Crump's cat, Muffin, is always there. She will make your visit fun!

Write a word from the ad to complete each sentence. Choose from the words in dark type.

1. Have you ever _____ a toy in Mr. Crump's Toy Shop?

2. A toy _____ can take off and land.

3. You must _____ that toy to make it go.

4. This toy can _____ up high.

5. Mr. Crump's Toy Shop sells lots of _____.

Directed Reading

Page 62 Read the title of the story aloud, and have children repeat it. Ask what a promise is. Then have children discuss the picture. Explain that Mr. Crump owns a toy shop. Have children read page 62 to find out more about the picture. **Who is the boy in the picture?** (*Lun*) INFERENTIAL: DRAW CONCLUSIONS **What do the boy and his mom buy?** (*a toy plane*) LITERAL: NOTE DETAILS

Page 63 Ask children what toy they see in the picture on page 63. If necessary, explain that a crane is used to lift heavy things. Then have children read page 63. Ask: **Which crane do Bud and his dad buy?** (*the one Mr. Crump is pointing to*) INFERENTIAL: INTERPRET STORY EVENTS **Why do Bud and his dad get that one?** (*because its engine works; because it has directions*) INFERENTIAL: CAUSE AND EFFECT

Page 64 Ask what animal children see in the picture on page 64 and whether they think it is a toy or real. Then have them read page 64 to find out. **Who is Muffin?** (*She is Mr. Crump's cat.*) LITERAL: NOTE DETAILS **What does Muffin hear?** (*a buzz from a bug*) INFERENTIAL: DRAW CONCLUSIONS **What do you think Muffin will do next?** (Possible response: *I think she will chase the bug because she likes bugs.*) INFERENTIAL: MAKE PREDICTIONS

Page 65 Have children read page 65. Ask: **What does Muffin do?** (*She runs after the bug.*) INFERENTIAL: USE PICTURE AND CONTEXT CLUES **What can Muffin do? What can the bug do?** (*Muffin can run, and the bug can fly.*) LITERAL: NOTE DETAILS **Do you think that Muffin will get the bug?** (Possible response: *Mr. Crump promises that Muffin will get it, so she probably will.*) INFERENTIAL: MAKE PREDICTIONS

Page 66 Read the first four sentences on page 66. Ask: **What happens to the plane?** (*It smashes; it is flat.*) LITERAL: NOTE DETAILS **What do the bug and Muffin land on next? What happens?** (*They land on the shelf, and the toys fall down.*) LITERAL: SEQUENCE **Why is Muffin digging?** (Possible answer: *She is looking for the bug.*) UNDERSTAND CHARACTERS' ACTIONS

Page 67 Have children read page 67. Ask: **Does Muffin get the bug?** (*yes*) **What does she do with it?** (*She gives it to Mr. Crump.*) LITERAL: NOTE DETAILS **What happens to the bug?** (*Mr. Crump lets it go, and it flies away.*) INFERENTIAL: INTERPRET STORY EVENTS

Page 68 Have children find Muffin in the picture on page 68. Ask what they think Muffin will do next. Then have children read page 68 to find out. **What do you think Muffin will do next? Why?** (Possible response: *She will probably chase the bug, because she likes to hunt for bugs.*) INFERENTIAL: MAKE PREDICTIONS **What do you think will happen to the store?** (Possible response: *It will get messy again.*) INFERENTIAL: MAKE PREDICTIONS

SUMMARIZING THE SELECTION Ask children to act out the story. Then help them summarize the story in a few sentences. INFERENTIAL: SUMMARIZE

Answers to Think About It Questions

Page 69 1. Mr. Crump promised that Muffin would get her bug. SUMMARY
2. Accept reasonable responses, such as: No, because some bugs may move faster than Muffin. INTERPRETATION
3. Accept reasonable responses. TASK

Name ______________________

REPRODUCIBLE STUDENT ACTIVITY PAGE

The Promise

Read the sentences. Write a word to complete each one. Use the words to retell the first part of the story.

1. Lun asks Mr. Crump if the ________ **bug plane cat** will go.	**2.** Lun and his mom ________ **lost bent bought** the toy.
3. Bud asks Mr. Crump if the crane will ________. **start lift stop**	**4.** Muffin is Mr. Crump's ________. **bug toy cat**

Use words from the box to answer these questions. Write your answers on the lines to retell the rest of the story.

toys	**bug**	**fly**

5. What did Bud's dad say a bug can do? ________

6. What spilled over in the shop when Muffin jumped at the bug? ________

7. What did Muffin see at the end of the story? ________

Too Many Cupcakes

by Deborah Eaton **Use with *Blue Skies*, pages 70–77.**

Preteaching Skills: Digraphs /th/*th*, /hw/*wh*

Teach/Model

IDENTIFY THE SOUND Have children say the following sentence three times: *I whacked my thumb when I ran on a thin path.* Have children identify the words with the /th/ sound. (*thumb, thin, path*) Then have them identify the words with the /hw/ sound. (*whacked, when*)

ASSOCIATE LETTERS TO THEIR SOUNDS Write on the board the sentence *I whacked my thumb when I ran on a thin path.* Underline the digraph *th* in *thumb, thin,* and *path.* Tell children that the letters *th* can stand for the /th/ sound they hear in *thumb, thin,* and *path.* Then underline the digraph *wh* in *whacked* and *when.* Tell children that the letters *wh* can stand for the /hw/ sound they hear in *whacked* and *when.*

WORD BLENDING Write the words *thing, think, whisk,* and *whip* on the board. Point to *thing.* Model blending the sounds to read *thing*: Slide your hand under the letters as you slowly elongate the sounds. Then read the word naturally. Have children practice blending the sounds in each of the other words to read each word aloud.

Practice/Apply

APPLY THE SKILL *Consonant Substitution* Write each of the following words on the board, and have children read it aloud. Make the changes necessary to form the word in parentheses. Have children read aloud each new word.

tin (thin)	hen (when)	wit (with)	mop (moth)
tick (thick)	risk (whisk)	pat (path)	mat (math)

DICTATION AND WRITING Have children number a sheet of paper 1–8. Dictate the following words, and have children write them. After they have finished, write each word on the board so children can proofread their work. On their paper, they should draw a line through a misspelled word and write the correct spelling above it.

1. whiz*	2. when	3. whisk	4. thud*	*Word appears in
5. thick	6. bath*	7. math	8. cloth	"Too Many Cupcakes."

Dictate the following sentence: *When will a moth get in a bath?*

READ LONGER WORDS *Review Compound Words* Write the word *bathtub* on the board. Remind children that when they see a longer word, they should look for smaller words in it. Model the strategy with the word *bathtub.* Cover the word *tub* and have children read aloud the remaining word. Then cover the word *bath* and have children read aloud the remaining word. Draw your hand under the entire word as children read it aloud. Follow a similar procedure for the words *without* and *thumbtack.*

REPRODUCIBLE STUDENT ACTIVITY PAGE

INDEPENDENT PRACTICE See the reproducible Student Activity on page 51.

Too Many Cupcakes

Read the story. Circle all the words with *wh* or *th*.

Seth Makes Broth

Seth makes broth. He wants
his broth to be thick.
Seth has some broth. It is not
thick. It is thin!

Seth whips up an egg. He adds
an egg to his broth.
Now his broth is thick. Seth
is glad.

Circle and write the word that best completes each sentence.

1. Seth makes _____.

               whip   broth   path

2. Seth likes _____ broth.

           bath   when   thick

3. The broth Seth makes is _____.

                  tin   thin   with

4. Seth _____ up an egg.

    whips   with   wishes

5. Now the broth is _____.

         thick   both   when

Harcourt

Introducing Vocabulary

Apply word identification strategies.

IDENTIFY VOCABULARY WORDS Display the vocabulary words, and have children identify words they know. Remind children that looking for spelling patterns can help them read new words. Ask children to use what they know about the CVC spelling pattern to help them read the word *mess* aloud. Then point to each of the other words and read it aloud. Have children read it aloud after you.

Check understanding.

Discuss the meaning of the vocabulary words with children. Then ask them to write the vocabulary words on a sheet of paper. Have children name the word that completes each sentence and then circle it on their papers.

VOCABULARY DEFINED
bowl a round, deep dish that can be used for mixing
door a big piece of wood or metal used to close or open an entrance
kitchen a room used for cooking and eating
knock to rap or pound on a door
mess a state of disorder
oven the part of a stove used for baking

- I heard someone ___. *(knock)*
- I opened the ___ to see who was there. *(door)*
- My friend Stan came into the ___ to help me bake a cake. *(kitchen)*
- We mixed everything in a big ___. *(bowl)*
- Then we baked our cake in the hot ___. *(oven)*
- Finally, we cleaned up our baking ___. *(mess)*

Children may be unfamiliar with some of the words in the title of the selection that they will read. Distribute the vocabulary page, point to the title, "Too Many Cupcakes," read it aloud, and have children read it with you.

REPRODUCIBLE STUDENT ACTIVITY PAGE

INDEPENDENT PRACTICE See the reproducible Student Activity on page 53.

NOTE: The following vocabulary words from "Hedgehog Bakes a Cake" are reinforced in "Too Many Cupcakes." If children are unfamiliar with these words, point them out as you encounter them during reading: *recipe, buttery, yellow cake* (p. 71); *batter* (p. 72); *smeared* (p. 73); and *perfect* (p. 74).

Too Many Cupcakes

Look at the picture. Draw a line from each word in the box to where you see it in the picture.

bowl	door	kitchen	knock	mess	oven

Write a word from the box to complete each sentence.

1. Rabbit was in his _____.

2. His friends had made a big _____.

3. A big _____ fell down and broke.

4. Broken eggs were on the hot _____.

5. Just then, there was a _____. "Who is it?" called Rabbit.

6. Possum was at the _____. "I'm here to help!" he said.

Harcourt

Directed Reading

Page 70
Read the title of the story aloud. Point out Rabbit and Possum in the picture. Then have children read page 70. Ask: **What will Rabbit and Possum do?** (*make cupcakes*) INFERENTIAL: DRAW CONCLUSIONS **Why might Possum think cupcakes are grand?** (Accept reasonable responses.) CRITICAL: EXPRESS OPINIONS

Page 71
Read aloud the first two sentences on page 71. Then have children read to find out why Rabbit is a whiz in the kitchen and Possum is not. **Why is Rabbit a whiz in the kitchen?** (Possible response: *Rabbit gets the recipe; Rabbit knows what to do.*) INFERENTIAL: UNDERSTAND CHARACTERS' TRAITS **Why is Possum not a whiz in the kitchen?** (*He drops the bowl and makes a mess.*) INFERENTIAL: UNDERSTAND CHARACTERS' TRAITS **Why do you think Rabbit says "the bathtub"?** (Possible response: *Maybe they will mix the batter in the bathtub.*) INFERENTIAL: MAKE PREDICTIONS

Page 72
Have children discuss the picture. Then have them read page 72 to find out if their predictions about the bathtub are right. Ask: **Why does Rabbit say "The bathtub"?** (*He uses the bathtub as a big bowl because the big bowl broke.*) INFERENTIAL: CONFIRM PREDICTIONS **How does Possum make a mess this time?** (*He falls into the batter in the tub.*) INFERENTIAL: INTERPRET STORY EVENTS

Page 73
Have children read page 73 to find out whether Rabbit gets angry. **Do you think Rabbit feels angry at Possum?** (Possible response: *No. He just wants Possum to help put the cupcakes into the oven.*) INFERENTIAL: UNDERSTAND CHARACTERS' EMOTIONS **What do you think will happen next?** (Accept reasonable responses.) INFERENTIAL: MAKE PREDICTIONS

Page 74
Have children discuss the picture on page 74. Then have them read to find out why the oven door is open. Ask: **Why is the oven door a little bit open?** (*to cook the batter that is on Possum*) INFERENTIAL: CAUSE AND EFFECT **Why do you think Rabbit says "Perfect!"?** (Possible response: *He thinks the cupcakes and the batter on Possum are ready to eat.*) INFERENTIAL: INTERPRET STORY EVENTS

Page 75
Have children read page 75 to find why Possum is sad. Ask: **Why is Possum sad at first?** (*He doesn't think that he is a whiz in the kitchen; he feels bad that he always makes a mess.*) INFERENTIAL: IDENTIFY CHARACTERS' EMOTIONS **Do you think Possum is still sad at the end? Why or why not?** (Possible response: *No, because Rabbit says it's OK and that Possum will be a whiz at eating them.*) INFERENTIAL: DRAW CONCLUSIONS

SUMMARIZING THE SELECTION Have children make stick puppets of Rabbit and Possum. Ask them to use the puppets to retell the story. Then help them summarize the story in a few sentences. INFERENTIAL: SUMMARIZE

Answers to Think About It Questions

Page 76
1. Rabbit mixed the cake batter in the bathtub. Possum dropped the big bowl that Rabbit had planned to use. SUMMARY
2. Possum was sad because he wasn't much help in the kitchen. INTERPRETATION
3. Accept reasonable responses. Children's responses should reflect an understanding of story concepts. TASK

Page 77
For instruction on the Focus Skill: Synonyms and Antonyms, see page 77 in *Blue Skies.*

Name _____

Too Many Cupcakes

Answer the questions below to tell about "Too Many Cupcakes."

Who was a whiz in the kitchen, Possum or Rabbit? _____	Who let the bowl land with a crash? _____
What did Rabbit and Possum mix in the bathtub? _____	Who fell into the bathtub? _____
How did the hot oven help Possum? *It cooked the batter on Possum.*	What can Possum do with the cupcakes? *Eat them.*

What do you like best in the story?
Responses will vary.
_____
_____
_____
_____

Harcourt

A Lemonade Surprise

by Julia Miguel   **Use with *Blue Skies*, pages 78–85.**

Preteaching Skills: *R*-Controlled Vowel /är/*ar*

Teach/Model

IDENTIFY THE SOUND Have children repeat the following sentence three times: *It is hard to park a car in the dark.* Ask children which words in the sentence have the /är/ sound. (*hard, park, car, dark*)

ASSOCIATE LETTERS TO THEIR SOUNDS Write this sentence on the board: *It is hard to park a car in the dark.* Underline the letters *ar* in *hard, park, car,* and *dark.* Tell children that the letters *ar* stand for the /är/ sound they hear in *hard, park, car,* and *dark.* Have children repeat the words.

WORD BLENDING Write *car* on the board and underline the *ar.* Model blending the sounds to read *car:* Slide your hand under the word as you slowly elongate the sounds. Then read the word naturally. Have children practice blending sounds to read these words aloud: *bar, part,* and *lark.*

Practice/Apply

APPLY THE SKILL *Vowel Substitution* Write each of the following words on the board, and have children read it aloud. Make the changes necessary to form the word in parentheses. Have children read each new word.

had (hard)	lad (lard)	ham (harm)	ban (barn)
pack (park)	cat (cart)	pat (part)	mat (mart)

DICTATION AND WRITING Have children number a sheet of paper 1–7. Dictate the following words, and have children write them. After they write each word, write it on the board so children can proofread their work. On their papers, they should draw a line through a misspelled word and write the correct spelling below it.

1. yard*	2. yarn	3. card*	4. star
5. park	6. start	7. farm	

Word appears in "A Lemonade Surprise."

Then dictate the following sentence: *The car is parked in the barn.*

READ LONGER WORDS *Introduce VCCV* Write *market* on the board. Tell children that they can often figure out longer words by looking for parts they know. Cover the *ket* in *market.* Have children read the word part that is left. (*mar*) Then follow a similar procedure to have children read *ket.* Model how to blend the two parts together to read *market.* Then read the word naturally. Follow a similar procedure to have children blend word parts to read *target* and *carpet.*

REPRODUCIBLE STUDENT ACTIVITY PAGE

....

INDEPENDENT PRACTICE See the reproducible Student Activity on page 57.

A Lemonade Surprise

Circle the word that makes the sentence tell about the picture. Then write the word.

1. "It is time to go. Let's get in the

_____ ," said Mom.

barn   **car**   **cat**

2. We got a snack at the

_____ .

farm   **barn**   **market**

3. It was not _____

    far   **yard**   **fat**

to the park.

4. I got up on the _____ .

    bars   **jars**   **harm**

5. It was _____

    had   **hard**   **tar**

to find Mark when he hid.

6. We left the park when it got

_____ .

    wet   **dark**   **cart**

7. We had fun at the _____ !

    park   **farm**   **pack**

Harcourt

Introducing Vocabulary

Apply word identification strategies.

IDENTIFY VOCABULARY WORDS Display the vocabulary words, and ask children to identify words they know. Remind children that knowing the sounds that letters stand for can help them read new words. Point to each vocabulary word, and read it aloud. Have children read it after you.

Check understanding.

Discuss the meanings of the vocabulary words. Then ask children to write the vocabulary words on a sheet of paper. Have children name the word that answers each of the following questions and then circle that word on their papers.

Which word . . .

- **describes a glass with nothing in it?** *(empty)*
- **tells what you need to buy things at the store?** *(money)*
- **means "not right"?** *(wrong)*
- **names a place where a group of children might gather?** *(clubhouse)*
- **completes this sentence:** *The store was crowded, and ___ were great!* *(sales)*

Children may be unfamiliar with some of the words in the title of the selection that they will read. After distributing the vocabulary page, point to the title, "A Lemonade Surprise," read it aloud, and have children read it with you.

REPRODUCIBLE STUDENT ACTIVITY PAGE

INDEPENDENT PRACTICE See the reproducible Student Activity on page 59.

NOTE: The following vocabulary words from "Lemonade for Sale" are reinforced in "A Lemonade Surprise." If children are unfamiliar with these words, point them out as you encounter them during reading: *glum* (p. 78); *announced, rebuild* (p. 80); *stand, members* (p. 81); and *arrived* (p. 83).

A Lemonade Surprise

Read the sentences. Write a word from the box to complete each sentence.

money   clubhouse   sales wrong   empty

1. Barb saw some kids in the next yard. "What's

_____?" she asked. "You look sad."

2. "Our _____ fell down," Mark said.

3. "We need a lot of _____ to fix it."

4. Barb gave the kids something to drink.
"We can sell this!" they said. "If we have a lot of

_____, we can fix the clubhouse."

5. Barb and the kids made lots of the drink. When all the cups

were _____ , the kids stopped selling.

Do you know what the kids were selling? Read "A Lemonade Surprise" and find out.

Harcourt

Directed Reading

Page 78 Read aloud the title of the story. Explain that children will find out what the surprise is as they read the story. Then read page 78 aloud. Ask: **What does glum mean?** (*sad; unhappy*) INFERENTIAL: USE CONTEXT CLUES **Why is Barb glum?** (*She has recently moved and misses her friends.*) INFERENTIAL: IDENTIFY CHARACTERS' EMOTIONS/DRAW CONCLUSIONS

Page 79 Read aloud the first sentence on page 79. Then have children read the rest of the page to find out what Barb does next. Ask: **What does Barb do after she sees the kids?** (*She takes lemonade next door to share.*) INFERENTIAL: SEQUENCE **What do you think will happen when Barb gets next door?** (Accept reasonable responses.) INFERENTIAL: MAKE PREDICTIONS

Page 80 Write the words *announced* and *rebuild* on the board, and read them aloud. Have children read page 80 to find out what someone announced and what the kids want to rebuild. Ask: **Do the kids like the lemonade?** (*yes*) INFERENTIAL: DRAW CONCLUSIONS **What does Mark announce?** (*that the pile of wood was a clubhouse that fell down*) LITERAL: NOTE DETAILS **Why can't the kids rebuild the clubhouse?** (*They have no money.*) INFERENTIAL: CAUSE AND EFFECT

Page 81 Have children read page 81 to find out what the kids decide to do. Ask: **What do the club members decide to do?** (*set up a lemonade stand to make money*) LITERAL: NOTE DETAILS **How do you think they got their idea?** (Possible response: *from the lemonade that Barb brought*) INFERENTIAL: UNDERSTAND CHARACTERS' MOTIVES

Page 82 Ask children to read page 82 to find out what the club members do to get started. **What do Karl and Kim do?** (*set up the stand*) LITERAL: NOTE DETAILS **What do Barb and Mark do?** (*make lemonade*) LITERAL: NOTE DETAILS **Do you think the kids will make money?** (Accept reasonable responses.) INFERENTIAL: MAKE PREDICTIONS

Page 83 Have children read page 83 to find out whether the lemonade stand is a success. **Was the lemonade stand a success? How do you know?** (*Yes, because the kids make enough money to rebuild the clubhouse.*) INFERENTIAL: INTERPRET STORY EVENTS

Page 84 Have children read page 84 to find out whether Barb will be allowed in the clubhouse. Ask: **What does the clubhouse sign say?** (*Just Members*) LITERAL: NOTE DETAILS **Why does Barb feel glum again?** (Possible response: *She is not a club member, and only members are allowed in the clubhouse.*) INFERENTIAL: UNDERSTAND CHARACTERS' FEELINGS **How does Barb feel at the end? Why?** (*She is happy because she is a friend, and all friends are club members.*) INFERENTIAL: INTERPRET STORY EVENTS

SUMMARIZING THE SELECTION Ask students to think about Barb's problem and how she solved it, and the kids' problem and how they solved it. Then have them summarize the story in a few sentences. INFERENTIAL: SUMMARIZE

Answers to Think About It Questions

Page 85
1. Barb brings some lemonade to the kids next door. She helps them make money for a new clubhouse. SUMMARY
2. Barb misses her friends, and her mother says that she will make new friends at school. INTERPRETATION
3. Accept reasonable responses. TASK

A Lemonade Surprise

Read the clues. Then complete the puzzle with words from the box.

clubhouse	empty	sales	wrong	money

Across

2. Many people bought lemonade, so _____ were good.

4. When Barb was sad, her mom asked, "What's _____?"

5. At last, the lemonade jug was _____.

Down

1. The kids wanted to rebuild the _____.

3. Barb added up the _____.

Write what you liked best about the story. Use as many words from the box as you can.

Responses will vary.

_____

_____

_____

_____

Anna's Apple Dolls

by Meish Goldish　　　　　**Use with *Blue Skies*, pages 86–93.**

Preteaching Skills: Digraphs /ch/ch, tch

Teach/Model

IDENTIFY THE SOUND Have children repeat the following sentence three times: *Charlie the Chimp can catch Chuck the Chick.* Ask children which words in the sentence have the /ch/ sound. (*Charlie, Chimp, catch, Chuck, Chick*)

ASSOCIATE LETTERS TO THEIR SOUNDS Write on the board the sentence *Charlie the Chimp can catch Chuck the Chick.* Underline the words *Charlie, Chimp, Chuck,* and *Chick.* Ask how the words are alike. (*begin with ch*) Tell children that the letters *ch* often stand for the /ch/ sound that they hear at the beginning of *Charlie, Chimp, Chuck,* and *Chick.* Then underline the letters *tch* in *catch.* Explain that these letters also stand for /ch/.

WORD BLENDING Write the word *chat* on the board and underline the *ch.* Model blending the sounds to read *chat:* Slide your hand under the word as you slowly elongate the sounds. Then read the word naturally. Have children practice blending sounds to read these words: *chip, chop, itch, patch.*

Practice/Apply

APPLY THE SKILL *Consonant Substitution* Write each of the following words on the board, and have children read it aloud. Make the changes necessary to form the word in parentheses. Have children read each new word.

cat (chat)	mop (chop)	cap (catch)	swim (switch)
tin (chin)	west (chest)	ham (hatch)	pin (pitch)

DICTATION AND WRITING Have children number a sheet of paper 1–8. Write *chip* on the board and tell children that in the words you say, the /ch/ sound is spelled *ch,* as in *chip.* Dictate the words, and have children write them. After they write each word, write it on the board so children can proofread their work. On their papers, they should draw a line through a misspelled word and write the correct spelling above it.

1. chin*	2. chop*	3. chest	4. chart
5. chick	6. chat	7. such	8. much

*Word appears in "Anna's Apple Dolls."

Tell children that in the sentence, /ch/ will be spelled *tch.* Dictate the following sentence: *Mitch can match this batch.*

READ LONGER WORDS *Review Words with VCCV* Write the word *chipmunk* on the board. Remind children that they can look for word parts to help them read longer words. Cover *munk* and have children read the remaining word part. (*chip*) Follow a similar procedure to have them read *munk.* Help them blend the word parts to read *chipmunk.* Follow a similar procedure to have children blend word parts to read *chapter* and *charcoal.*

REPRODUCIBLE STUDENT ACTIVITY PAGE

INDEPENDENT PRACTICE See the reproducible Student Activity on page 63.

Name _____

Anna's Apple Dolls

Fill in the oval in front of the sentence that tells about the picture.

1 ◯ The chick has an itch on its chest.
   ◯ The cat has an itch on its chin.
   ◯ The cat has an itch on its back.

2 ◯ Dan can stitch the patch.
   ◯ Dan can catch a fast pitch.
   ◯ We will switch the chart.

3 ◯ Mitch is catching a fish.
   ◯ Anna can pitch fast.
   ◯ Anna is catching that ball.

4 ◯ Ben and Sam chat by the ditch.
   ◯ Ben and Sam pitch in the kitchen.
   ◯ Ben and Sam chat in the kitchen.

5 ◯ Chen and Pat have matching patches.
   ◯ Chen and Pat have matching charms.
   ◯ Chen and Pat have matching charts.

6 ◯ Mitch is stitching a patch.
   ◯ Mitch is catching a pitch.
   ◯ Mitch is switching his hat.

Harcourt

Introducing Vocabulary

Apply word
identification
strategies.

IDENTIFY VOCABULARY WORDS Display the vocabulary words, and ask children to identify words they know. Remind children that they can sometimes figure out an unfamiliar word by looking for familiar word parts or spelling patterns. Point out the CVC(C) spelling pattern in *west* and the word parts in *cabin*. Ask children to use what they know about the CVC pattern and about looking for word parts to help them read these words aloud. Then point to each other word, and read it aloud. Have children read it aloud after you.

VOCABULARY DEFINED
cabin a small house, usually made of wood
family parents and their children
feet the things at the end of the legs
outdoors outside
seeds parts of a fruit from which new plants grow
west a direction that points to where the sun sets; the western part of the United States (the West)

Check
understanding.

Discuss the meanings of the vocabulary words. Then ask children to write the vocabulary words on a sheet of paper. Have children name the word that answers each of the following questions and circle that word on their papers.

- **What does a cat have four of?** *(feet)*
- **What do you see when you cut open an apple?** *(seeds)*
- **What is a small house built from logs?** *(cabin)*
- **What word is the opposite of *east*?** *(west)*
- **What word names a group of people?** *(family)*
- **Which word means "not inside"?** *(outdoors)*

Children may be unfamiliar with some of the words in the title of the selection that they will read. After distributing the vocabulary page, point to the title, "Anna's Apple Dolls," read it aloud, and have children read it with you.

**REPRODUCIBLE
STUDENT
ACTIVITY PAGE**

**INDEPENDENT
PRACTICE** See
the reproducible
Student Activity
on page 65.

NOTE: The following vocabulary words from "Johnny Appleseed" are reinforced in "Anna's Apple Dolls." If children are unfamiliar with these words, point them out as you encounter them during reading: *frontier* (p. 86), *orchard* (p. 87); *wild, nearby, survive, tame* (p. 89); and *which* (p. 91).

Name _____

Anna's Apple Dolls

Read the story.
Then fill in the web.

Anna and her **family** live in the **West.** Their home is a **cabin** made of logs.

Anna likes playing **outdoors** the best. She likes to play by the apple trees. She finds some apple **seeds** and a stick next to her **feet.** Anna has an idea. What do you think she will do?

Where do Anna and her family live?	**What kind of home does Anna live in?**
_____	_____
_____	_____
_____	_____

Anna

What does Anna like to do best?	**What does Anna find by the apple tree?**
_____	_____
_____	_____
	_____

Harcourt

Directed Reading

Pages 86–87 Read aloud the title on page 86. Tell children that "Anna's Apple Dolls" is a play that takes place many years ago in the old West. Ask children to discuss the picture on page 87 and to tell how it helps them know when and where the play takes place. Then ask children to read to find out what the girl, Anna, wants to do. **What does Anna want to do?** (*play in the apple orchard*) INFERENTIAL: UNDERSTAND CHARACTERS' MOTIVES **What does Anna's mother want Anna to do?** (*collect a big batch of apples*) INFERENTIAL: UNDERSTAND CHARACTERS' MOTIVES

Pages 88–89 Have children read page 89 to find out whom Anna meets on her way to the orchard.
Who does Anna meet? (*Charles, Kip, Mitch, and Garth*) LITERAL: NOTE DETAILS **How does Anna know them?** (*They are her older brothers.*) INFERENTIAL: DRAW CONCLUSIONS **How is Garth different from the other boys?** (Possible response: *He doesn't tease her, and he goes with her to the orchard.*) INFERENTIAL: COMPARE AND CONTRAST

Pages 90–91 Tell children to read page 91 to find out what Anna does with an apple.
What does Anna do with one of the apples? (*She makes it into an apple doll.*) INFERENTIAL: INTERPRET STORY EVENTS **What does Anna use to make the doll's eyes and mouth?** (*seeds*) INFERENTIAL: SYNTHESIZE **How does Anna make the doll's legs and feet?** (*with sticks*) LITERAL: NOTE DETAILS

Page 92 Have children read page 92 to find out what Anna's family thinks about her apple doll.
What does Anna's family think about her doll? (*They like it.*) INFERENTIAL: DRAW CONCLUSIONS **How are Anna's brothers different to her now from how they were before?** (Possible response: *First they were teasing her. Now they are being nice to her and complimenting her.*) INFERENTIAL: UNDERSTAND CHARACTERS' ACTIONS

SUMMARIZING THE SELECTION Ask children to think about what happened first, next, and last in "Anna's Apple Dolls." Then help children summarize the story in three sentences. (Possible response: *Anna's mom asks her to pick apples for the family. Anna uses an apple to make an apple doll. Anna's family likes her doll.*) INFERENTIAL: SUMMARIZE

Answers to Think About It Questions

Page 93 Read the page to children and have them discuss their responses to items 1 and 2. For the last item, brainstorm ideas with children before they begin to write or draw. Possible responses for items 1–3 are shown below.

1. Anna gets an apple. She uses seeds to make eyes and a mouth. She uses sticks for arms, legs, and feet. SUMMARY
2. They think she is just a little sister who can't do the hard work that they do. INTERPRETATION
3. Accept reasonable responses. TASK

Name _____

Anna's Apple Dolls

**Think about what happened in "Anna's Apple Dolls."
Write about the *beginning*, *middle*, and *end* of the
play. Use the words from the boxes in your answers.**

Beginning	cabin west

Where does the play happen?

_____

_____

What does Anna's mom ask her to do? | outdoors   apples |

_____

_____

Middle	seeds stick

What does Anna use to make her doll?

_____

_____

End	cabin family

Where does Anna take her doll? What happens there?

_____

_____

Harcourt

A Day in the Life of a Seed

by Jean Groce   **Use with *Blue Skies*, pages 94–101.**

Preteaching Skills: *R*-Controlled Vowel /ôr/or, ore, our

Teach/Model

IDENTIFY THE SOUND Have children repeat the following sentence three times: *Mort went to the store at four.* Have children identify the words in the sentence that have the /ôr/ sound. (*Mort, store, four*)

ASSOCIATE LETTERS TO THEIR SOUNDS Write on the board the sentence *Mort went to the store at four.* Underline the letters *or* in *Mort.* Tell children that the letters *or* often stand for the /ôr/ sound they hear in *Mort.* Have children repeat *Mort.* Then follow a similar procedure for *ore* (*store*) and *our* (*four*).

WORD BLENDING Write *sport* on the board. Model blending the sounds to read *sport:* Slide your hand under the word as you slowly elongate the sounds. Then read the word naturally. Have children practice blending sounds to read aloud these words: *corn, more, pour.*

Practice/Apply

APPLY THE SKILL *Vowel Substitution* Write each of the following words on the board, and have children read it aloud. Make the changes necessary to form the word in parentheses. Have children read each new word.

can (corn)	were (wore)	spot (sport)	far (four)
star (store)	par (pour)	bin (born)	hen (horn)

DICTATION AND WRITING Have children number a sheet of paper 1–8. Write *cork* on the board and tell children that in the words you say, the /ôr/ sound is spelled *or* as in *cork.* Dictate the words, and have children write them. After they have finished, write each word on the board so children can proofread their work. Have them draw a line through a misspelled word and write the correct spelling below it.

1. for*	2. sport	3. porch	4. morning*	*Word appears in "A Day*
5. forming*	6. short*	7. corn*	8. fork	*in the Life of a Seed."*

Tell children that in the following sentence, /ôr/ will be spelled *our.* Dictate the sentence: *It started to pour on your dad at four.*

READ LONGER WORDS *Review Compound Words* Write the word *forgot* on the board. Remind children that they can often figure out longer words by looking for shorter words in them. Cover *got* and have children read the smaller word. (*for*) Follow a similar procedure to have them read *got.* Model how to blend the smaller words to read aloud the longer word *forgot.* Follow a similar procedure to have children blend smaller words to read these longer words: *shortstop* and *corncob.*

REPRODUCIBLE STUDENT ACTIVITY PAGE

INDEPENDENT PRACTICE See the reproducible Student Activity on page 69.

A Day in the Life of a Seed

Look at the picture. Then do what the sentences tell you.

1. Bob, Cora, and Tim are on the team with the red shorts. Make their shorts red.

2. Peg, Mort, and Greg are on the team with the black shorts. Make Greg's shorts black.

3. Tim wants to score more runs. Give him a bat.

4. The team in the red shorts scored four runs. Put a four in the score box.

5. Peg forgot her cap. Give her a cap.

6. Mort is pitching for the team with the black shorts. Give him a ball.

7. Greg is not playing the right sport. Put an X on his club.

Now circle the words above that have *or*, *ore*, and *our*.

Introducing Vocabulary

Apply word identification strategies.

IDENTIFY VOCABULARY WORDS Display the vocabulary words, and ask children to identify the words that they know. Remind children that knowing spelling patterns can help them figure out an unfamiliar word. Point out the consonant blends and CVC pattern in *plant*. Ask children to use what they know about the CVC pattern to help them read this word aloud. Then point to each of the other words as you read it aloud. Have children read it aloud after you.

Check understanding.

Discuss the meanings of the vocabulary words. Then ask children to write the vocabulary words on a sheet of paper. Have children name the word that answers each of the following questions and circle that word on their papers.

VOCABULARY DEFINED
flowers the colorful, blooming parts of a plant
plant a living thing that grows from the ground
roots parts of plants that grow downward under the ground
soil the ground in which plants grow
sprout to begin to grow

Which word . . .

- means "to begin to grow"? *(sprout)*
- is another word for *dirt*? *(soil)*
- tells which part of a plant grows into the ground? *(roots)*
- tells what roses and daisies are? *(flowers)*
- tells what a tree, a bush, or a flower is? *(plant)*

Children may be unfamiliar with some of the words in the title of the selection that they will read. After distributing the vocabulary page, point to the title, "A Day in the Life of a Seed," read it aloud, and have children read it with you.

REPRODUCIBLE STUDENT ACTIVITY PAGE

INDEPENDENT PRACTICE See the reproducible Student Activity on page 71.

NOTE: The following vocabulary words from "From Seed to Plant" are reinforced in "A Day in the Life of a Seed." If children are unfamiliar with these words, point them out as you encounter them during reading: *protects, ripens* (p. 95); *stream* (p. 96); *nutrition* (p. 99); and *beautiful* (p. 100).

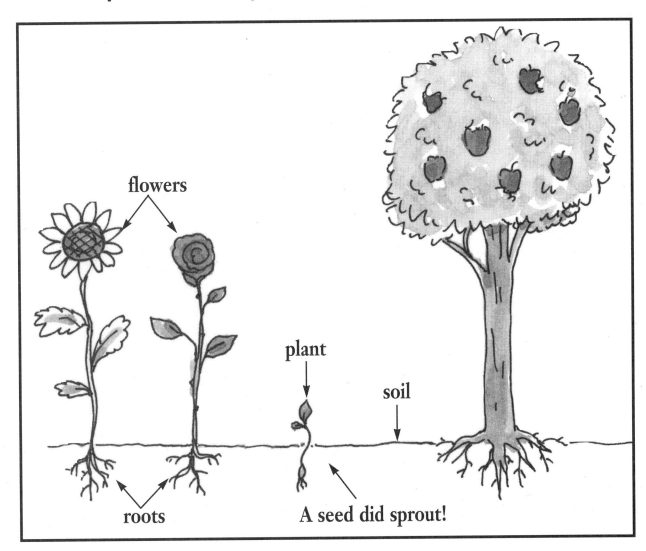

Name _____

A Day in the Life of a Seed

Read the sentence and words in the picture. Then write a word from the picture to complete each sentence.

flowers

plant

soil

roots

A seed did sprout!

1. There are two _____ in this garden.

2. The _____ are down in the _____.

3. Soon, you can see the seed begin to _____.

4. It will grow into a tall, green _____.

Harcourt

Directed Reading

Pages 94–95 Read aloud the title. Ask children to describe what they see in the picture on pages 94–95. Ask children what they think this selection will be about. Then have them read to find out what is happening in the sunflowers. **What is happening in the sunflowers?** (*Seeds are forming in them.*) LITERAL: NOTE DETAILS   **What happens when the pod splits?** (*A sunflower seed pops out.*) LITERAL: NOTE SEQUENCE   **What do you think will happen to the seed?** (Accept reasonable responses.) INFERENTIAL: MAKE PREDICTIONS

Page 96 Have children read page 96 to find out what happens to the seed. **What happens to the seed?** (*A mouse picks it up and drops it into a stream.*) LITERAL: NOTE DETAILS   **What do you think will happen to the seed now?** (Accept reasonable responses.) INFERENTIAL: MAKE PREDICTIONS

Page 97 Have children read page 97 to find out what happens to the seed. **What happens to the seed next?** (*It floats down the stream and then gets stuck in the grass and thorns.*) LITERAL: NOTE DETAILS   **What do you think will happen to the seed now?** (Accept reasonable responses.) INFERENTIAL: MAKE PREDICTIONS

Page 98 Have children read page 98 to find out what happens to the seed. **What happens to the seed now?** (*It falls into the soil when a rabbit pulls the grass out by the roots.*) LITERAL: NOTE DETAILS   **What do you think will happen next?** (*The seed will grow. It will not travel again because the trip is over.*) INFERENTIAL: DRAW CONCLUSIONS/ MAKE PREDICTIONS

Page 99 Have children read to find out the answer to the question, **What will happen now?** (*The seed will sprout; roots will form; a stem and leaves will grow.*) INFERENTIAL: SUMMARIZE

Page 100 Have children look at the picture on page 100. Ask what they think the seed will grow into and what will happen after it does. Model as necessary: **I think the seed will grow into a sunflower that will produce more seeds that will grow into more sunflowers.** Then have children read the page to find out if they were right. INFERENTIAL: UNDERSTAND STORY EVENTS

SUMMARIZING THE SELECTION Ask children to think about the trip the seed in this story takes. Then have them summarize the story in a few sentences. INFERENTIAL: SUMMARIZE

Answers to Think About It Questions

Page 101 1. First it drops from the pod. Then a mouse picks it up and drops it into a stream. It floats until it gets stuck in some grass. A rabbit pulls up the grass, and the seed falls into the soil. SUMMARY
2. Roots begin to grow. Then a stem and leaves grow. Soon the seed becomes a new plant. INTERPRETATION
3. Accept reasonable responses, but they should tell the mouse's part in the seed's travels. TASK

Name _____

A Day in the Life of a Seed

Complete the sentences with words from the box to tell what happens in "A Day in the Life of a Seed."

sprout	plant	soil	flowers	roots

1. The garden has lots of tall, yellow _____.

2. A rabbit pulls up grass. The seed falls to the _____.

3. The seed will start to _____.

4. First, _____ will form and go down into the soil.

5. Soon it becomes a tall _____.

Write what you liked best about the story. Use as many words from the box as you can.

_____

_____

_____

_____

_____

Phonics

Mr. Carver's Carrots

by Cassidy James   Use with *Blue Skies*, pages 102–109.

Preteaching Skills: Vowel Diphthong /ou/ou, ow

Teach/Model

IDENTIFY THE SOUND Have children repeat the following sentence three times: *How did a brown sprout come out of the ground?* Ask children which words in the sentence have the /ou/ sound. (*How, brown, sprout, out, ground*)

ASSOCIATE LETTERS TO THEIR SOUNDS Write on the board the sentence *How did a brown sprout come out of the ground?* Circle the words *sprout, out,* and *ground,* and ask how they are alike. (*the letters ou*) Underline the letters *ou* in each of the circled words. Tell children that the letters *ou* often stand for the /ou/ sound they hear in *sprout, out* and *ground.* Have children repeat each word and listen for the /ou/ sound. Then follow a similar procedure with the letters *ow* in *How* and *brown.*

WORD BLENDING Write *shout* on the board. Model blending sounds to read *shout:* Slide your hand under the word as you slowly elongate the sounds. Then read the word naturally. Have children practice blending sounds to read aloud these words: *round, clown, now.*

Practice/Apply

APPLY THE SKILL *Vowel Substitution* Write each of the following words on the board, and have children read it aloud. Make the changes necessary to form the word in parentheses. Have a volunteer read each new word.

we (wow)	led (loud)	den (down)	moth (mouth)	clan (clown)
car (cow)	put (pout)	pond (pound)	sand (sound)	fund (found)

DICTATION AND WRITING Have children number a sheet of paper 1–8. Write the word *out* on the board and tell children that in the words you say, the /ou/ sound is spelled *ou,* as in *out.* Dictate the words, and have children write them. After they write each word, write it on the board so children can proofread their work. On their papers, they should draw a line through a misspelled word and write the correct spelling above it.

1. loud	2. shout	3. sounds*	4. cloud	*Word appears in
5. ground*	6. sprouts*	7. proud	8. count	"Mr. Carver's Carrots."

Tell children that in the following sentence, /ow/ will be spelled *ow.* Dictate the sentence: *The brown cow will go down to the town.*

READ LONGER WORDS *Review Ending* **-ing** Write the word *shouting* on the board. Remind children that they can often figure out longer words by looking for parts they already know. Cover the *-ing* ending, and have children read *shout.* Follow a similar procedure to have them read the ending *-ing.* Model how to blend the parts to read aloud the longer word *shouting.* Follow a similar procedure to have children blend word parts to read these longer words: *plowing, frowning, sounding.*

REPRODUCIBLE STUDENT ACTIVITY PAGE

INDEPENDENT PRACTICE See the reproducible Student Activity on page 75.

Name _____

Mr. Carver's Carrots

Read the story. Circle all the words with the vowel sound you hear in *cow* and *found*.

At the Farm

Beth has a farm. Color her barn red. Color her house brown. Beth has four cows and a cat called Clown. Clown likes to run around.

Now Beth is plowing the ground. Clown has found a mouse. The mouse is about to fall down!

Now write a word with *ou* or *ow* to complete each sentence.

1. Beth's house is _____.

2. Beth has a cat and four _____.

3. Now Beth is plowing the _____.

4. The cat has _____ a mouse.

5. The mouse is about to fall _____.

Harcourt

Introducing Vocabulary

Apply word identification strategies.

Check understanding.

IDENTIFY VOCABULARY WORDS Display the vocabulary words, and ask children to identify the ones they know. Then remind children that knowing about the sounds that letters stand for can help them read new words. Then point to each vocabulary word. Read it aloud, and have children read it after you.

Discuss the meanings of the vocabulary words. Then ask children to write the vocabulary words on a sheet of paper. Have children name the word that answers each of the following questions, and circle that word on their papers.

VOCABULARY DEFINED
day the time between sunrise and sunset
floated rested on top of water
heat warmth
summer the season between spring and fall
waited was patient until something happened
watermelon a large fruit that has a green rind and is soft, red, and sweet inside

- **In what season is the month of July?** *(summer)*
- **What is it after the sun rises?** *(day)*
- **What is one thing the sun provides?** *(heat)*
- **What word tells what you did at the end of a long line?** *(waited)*
- **What means the opposite of *sank*?** *(floated)*
- **What is a kind of fruit?** *(watermelon)*

Children may be unfamiliar with some of the words in the title of the selection that they will read. After distributing the vocabulary page, point to the title, "Mr. Carver's Carrots," read it aloud, and have children read it with you.

REPRODUCIBLE STUDENT ACTIVITY PAGE

INDEPENDENT PRACTICE See the reproducible Student Activity on page 77.

NOTE: The following vocabulary words from "Watermelon Day" are reinforced in "Mr. Carver's Carrots." If children are unfamiliar with these words, point them out as you encounter them during reading: *wrinkled* (p. 102); *knelt, snug, beneath* (p. 103); *shimmered* and *relay race* (p. 105).

Mr. Carver's Carrots

Read each sentence. Write the word from the box that makes sense in the sentence.

watermelon	day	heat	waited	floated	summer

1. It was hot outside because it was _____.

2. The _____ from the sun wilted the flowers.

3. One _____, Ben was hungry for some carrots.

4. Ben planted carrot seeds. He _____ for the seeds to sprout.

5. At last! Ben could munch as he _____ on his pond.

6. Next, Ben wanted some _____.

Directed Reading

Page 102 Read aloud the title of the story. Point out Mr. Carver and Ben in the illustration. Then have children read page 102 to find out what Mr. Carver and Ben might do. Model a response: **Mr. Carver and Ben are hot. Mr. Carver wants to eat carrots, and Ben wishes they had planted carrots. The title is "Mr. Carver's Carrots." I think Mr. Carver and Ben will plant carrots.** INFERENTIAL: MAKE PREDICTIONS

Page 103 Have children read page 103 to find out what Mr. Carver and Ben do. Ask: **What does Mr. Carver do?** (*He gets carrot seeds and digs up the ground.*) LITERAL: NOTE DETAILS **What does Ben do?** (*He puts seeds in the soil and covers them with more soil.*) LITERAL: NOTE DETAILS **What does *snug beneath the soil* mean?** (*all covered up, or protected, under the soil*) INFERENTIAL: UNDERSTAND FIGURATIVE LANGUAGE

Page 104 Have children read page 104. Ask: **What happens after Ben plants the seeds?** (Possible response: *A storm comes and it rains.*) INFERENTIAL: SEQUENCE **How do you know that it rains hard?** (*Big drops plopped down fast and loudly.*) INFERENTIAL: UNDERSTAND DESCRIPTIVE LANGUAGE **What does Ben see outdoors?** (*little sprouts*) INFERENTIAL: DRAW CONCLUSIONS

Page 105 Have children read page 105. Ask: **What happens after the rain?** (*It gets very hot; there is a heat spell.*) INFERENTIAL: SEQUENCE **Why do Mr. Carver and Ben call what they do a "relay race to help the sprouts"?** (Possible response: *They are racing to keep the plants watered, and they are relaying because Ben is filling buckets and giving them to Mr. Carver to water the plants.*) INFERENTIAL: SPECULATE

Page 106 Have students read page 106. Ask: **What is the day that Mr. Carver and Ben had waited for?** (*the day when the carrots are ready to eat*) INFERENTIAL: INTERPRET STORY EVENTS **Do Mr. Carver and Ben like the carrots? How can you tell?** (*Yes. They crunch and munch the carrots.*) INFERENTIAL: DRAW CONCLUSIONS

Page 107 Have children read page 107. Ask: **What is Mr. Carver hungry for now?** (*watermelon*) LITERAL: NOTE DETAILS **How is the end of the story like the beginning?** (Possible response: *In both, Mr. Carver is hungry for something, and Mr. Carver and Ben ask what they are waiting for.*) INFERENTIAL: COMPARE AND CONTRAST

SUMMARIZING THE SELECTION Have children think about what happened first, next, and last in "Mr. Carver's Carrots." Help them summarize the story in three or four sentences. INFERENTIAL: SUMMARIZE

Answers to Think About It Questions

Page 108 1. They dig up the ground and put carrot seeds in the soil. Then they water the plants and wait for them to grow. SUMMARY
2. They water them. INTERPRETATION
3. Accept reasonable responses. TASK

Page 109 For instruction on the Focus Skill: Predict Outcomes, see page 109 in *Blue Skies.*

Mr. Carver's Carrots

These events are from "Mr. Carver's Carrots." They are out of order. Put a number in front of each one to show the right order.

_____   Mr. Carver and Ben munched on carrots.

_____   Mr. Carver and Ben pulled the carrots out of the ground.

_____   Sprouts came up after a storm.

_____   Ben put carrot seeds under the soil.

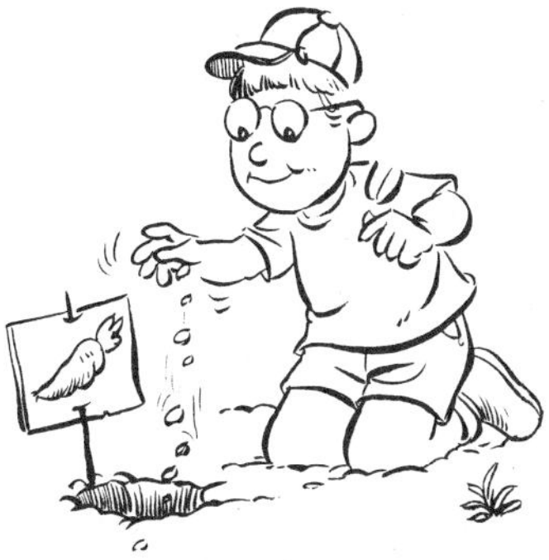

Now write each event in order. Put each one next to its number.

1. Ben put carrot seeds under the soil. _____

_____

2. Sprouts came up after a storm. _____

_____

3. Mr. Carver and Ben pulled the carrots out of the ground. _____

_____

4. Mr. Carver and Ben munched on carrots. _____

_____

While the Bear Sleeps

by Deborah Akers   Use with *Blue Skies*, pages 110–117.

Preteaching Skills: *R*-Controlled Vowel /ûr/ *er, ir, ur*

Teach/Model

IDENTIFY THE SOUND Have children repeat the following sentence three times: *Vern has a bird and a turtle.* Ask children to identify the words in the sentence that have the /ûr/ sound. (*Vern, bird, turtle*)

ASSOCIATE LETTERS TO THEIR SOUNDS Write on the board the sentence *Vern has a bird and a turtle.* Underline the letters *er* in *Vern, ir* in *bird*, and *ur* in *turtle*. Tell children that the letters *er, ir,* and *ur* often stand for the /ûr/ sound they hear in *Vern, bird,* and *turtle*. Have children repeat the words *Vern, bird,* and *turtle* and listen for the /ûr/ sound.

WORD BLENDING Write *shirt* on the board. Model blending the sounds to read *shirt:* Slide your hand under the word as you slowly elongate the sounds. Then read the word naturally. Have children practice blending sounds to read aloud these words: *turn, herd, surf,* and *firm*.

Practice/Apply

APPLY THE SKILL *Vowel Substitution* Write each of the following words on the board, and have children read it aloud. Make the changes necessary to form the word in parentheses. Have children read each new word.

hard (herd)	cub (curb)	hut (hurt)	torn (turn)	park (perk)
far (fur)	skit (skirt)	star (stir)	dart (dirt)	bud (bird)

DICTATION AND WRITING Have children number a sheet of paper 1–8. Write the word *girl* on the board and tell children that in the words you say, the /ûr/ sound is spelled *ir* as in *girl*. Dictate the words for children to write. After they write each word, write it on the board so children can proofread their work. On their papers, they should draw a line through a misspelled word and write the correct spelling below it.

1. bird*	2. skirt	3. first	4. dirt*	*Word appears in
5. swirls*	6. stir*	7. shirt	8. firm	"While the Bear Sleeps."

Tell children that in the following sentence, /ûr/ is spelled *er*. Dictate the sentence: *Her cat will perch on the rock with the fern.*

READ LONGER WORDS *Review Words with VCCV* Write the word *perfect* on the board. Remind children that they can often figure out longer words by looking for word parts that they know. Cover the *fect*, and have children read *per*. Follow a similar procedure to have them read *fect*. Model how to blend the word parts to read aloud the longer word *perfect*. Follow a similar procedure to have children blend the word parts to read these longer words: *stirring* and *sister*.

REPRODUCIBLE STUDENT ACTIVITY PAGE

INDEPENDENT PRACTICE See the reproducible Student Activity on page 81.

Directed Reading

Page 110 Read aloud the title of the story. Ask children what they know about bears and about things that happen while bears sleep. Have them use this information to fill in the first column in the chart on page 85. Then ask what children might like to learn from this selection. Have them use this discussion to help them fill in the second column of the chart. Then have children read page 110 to find out what the mouse does while the bear sleeps. **Where is the bear?** (*snug in his den*) LITERAL: NOTE DETAILS **What does the mouse do?** (*She digs in the ground to look for seeds that she hid in the dirt in autumn.*) INFERENTIAL: SUMMARIZE

Page 111 Discuss the meaning of the word *dusky.* (*dim or darkening*) Then have children read page 111 to find out what the mouse does at the dusky end of the day. **What does the mouse do at the end of the day?** (*She takes the seeds home and feeds her family.*) LITERAL: NOTE DETAILS **What will the bear do tomorrow?** (*The bear will probably continue sleeping.*) INFERENTIAL: MAKE PREDICTIONS

Page 112 Have children read page 112 to learn what the bird does while the bear sleeps. **What is the bird doing?** (*The bird is flying very far to look for food.*) INFERENTIAL: DRAW CONCLUSIONS **What does the bird find to eat?** (*red berries*) INFERENTIAL: INTERPRET STORY EVENTS

Page 113 Have children read page 113 to learn what the bird does at the dusky end of the day. **What does the bird do at the end of the day?** (*She rests.*) LITERAL: NOTE DETAILS **What does *stir* mean here?** (*move*) INFERENTIAL: USE CONTEXT CLUES

Page 114 Have children read page 114 to find out what the rabbit does while the bear sleeps. **What does the rabbit do while the bear sleeps?** (*He's searching for leaves to eat, and then he digs in the snow and finds some sprouts.*) INFERENTIAL: SUMMARIZE

Page 115 Have children read page 115 to find out what the rabbit does at the end of the day. **What does the rabbit do at the end of the day?** (*hops home*) LITERAL: NOTE DETAILS **Why will there be many more new plants for the rabbit to eat tomorrow?** (*because spring is coming and the snow is melting*) INFERENTIAL: INTERPRET STORY EVENTS **What will happen to the bear after the snow melts?** (*He will stir from his nap; he will wake up.*) INFERENTIAL: MAKE PREDICTIONS

Page 116 Have children read page 116 to find out what the bear will do when he knows a new day is beginning. **What will the bear do when he gets up?** (*He will probably look for food because he will be hungry.*) INFERENTIAL: MAKE PREDICTIONS

SUMMARIZING THE SELECTION Have children summarize the story by telling what the mouse, the bird, and the rabbit do while the bear is sleeping. INFERENTIAL: SUMMARIZE

Answers to Think About It Questions

Page 117
1. The mouse, the bird, and the rabbit have to work. SUMMARY
2. The bear sleeps during the winter and gets up in the spring. INTERPRETATION
3. Accept reasonable responses, which should include looking for food. TASK

Name _____

While the Bear Sleeps

Read the story. Circle the words with *er*, *ir*, or *ur*.

 A bird and a turtle met one day. "I can surf!" the turtle said.	 "Well, I can fly," said the bird. "Let's go up to my perch."
 "Let's go surfing," said the turtle. "No thanks," said the bird. "I do not want to surf. I will get my shirt wet."	 "As you like," said the turtle. "Now, will you get me back on firm ground? This perch is too far up for a turtle."

Circle the word to complete each sentence. Write it on the line.

1. A _____ and a turtle met one day.
   third   bird   perfect

2. The bird took the turtle to its _____.
   surf   perch   turn

3. The bird did not want to get its _____ wet.
   shirt   perch   dirt

4. The turtle wanted to get back on _____ ground.
   firm   term   first

Introducing Vocabulary

IDENTIFY VOCABULARY WORDS Display the vocabulary words, and ask children to identify the ones they know. Remind children that they can sometimes figure out an unfamiliar word by looking for familiar spelling or letter patterns. Point out the CVC pattern in *end* and *wind*. Ask children to use what they know about the CVC pattern to help them read these words. Follow a similar procedure with *or* and the word *morning*. Then have children find the two smaller words to help them read the longer word *today*.

Point to *beginning* and *tomorrow* in turn, and read each word aloud. Have children read it aloud after you.

Discuss the meanings of the vocabulary words. Then ask children to write the vocabulary words on a sheet of paper. Have children name the word that completes each of the following sentences and circle it on their papers.

> - **I wake up at 7:00 in the ___.** *(morning)*
> - **When something is starting, it is ___.** *(beginning)*
> - **A story is over at the ___.** *(end)*
> - **I will go the day after this one. I will go ___.** *(tomorrow)*
> - **I must work on this day. I must work ___.** *(today)*
> - **The ___ blew my hat away.** *(wind)*

Children may be unfamiliar with some of the words in the title of the selection that they will read. After distributing the vocabulary page, point to the title, "While the Bear Sleeps," read it aloud, and have children read it with you.

NOTE: The following vocabulary words from "When the Wind Stops" are reinforced in "While the Bear Sleeps." If children are unfamiliar with these words, point them out as you encounter them during reading: *autumn* (p. 110); *dusky, glowing, pointed* (p. 111); *completely* (p. 114); and *sliver* (p. 115).

<table>
<tr><td>VOCABULARY DEFINED</td></tr>
</table>

VOCABULARY DEFINED

beginning starting

end the last part

morning the first part of the day; from sunrise to noon

today this day

tomorrow the next day

wind air that is blowing

Name _____

While the Bear Sleeps

Read the ad.

> The mouse must dig for seeds this **morning**. The bear is snug in his den.
> Outdoors, a storm is **beginning**. A big **wind** swirls the snow.
> Will the mouse find the seeds **today**? Will the animals still be safe **tomorrow**? How will this story **end**?
> Read "While the Bear Sleeps" to find out!

Write a word from the ad to complete each sentence. Choose from the words in dark type.

1. A storm is _____.

2. A big _____ swirls the snow.

3. The mouse must find seeds _____.

4. Will the animals be safe _____?

5. At the _____ of the day, the sun will go down.

6. In the _____, the sun will come up.

Name _____

REPRODUCIBLE
STUDENT
ACTIVITY PAGE

While the Bear Sleeps

Fill in the first two parts of the chart before you read the story.

K	W	L
What I Know	**What I Want to Know**	**What I Learned**

After you read, answer these questions. Then, in the third part of the chart, write one thing you learned.

1. What is the bear doing? _____

_____

2. What are the mouse, the bird, and the rabbit doing? _____

_____

3. What will the bear do at the end of the story? _____

_____

Harcourt

Selection Comprehension • Grade 2   **85**

The Earth in Motion

by Kana Reilly   **Use with *Blue Skies*, pages 118–125.**

Preteaching Skills: Long Vowel /ā/a-e

Teach/Model

IDENTIFY THE SOUND Have children repeat the following sentence three times: *Dave can bake a cake for Pat.* Ask children which words in the sentence have the /ā/ sound they hear in *make*. (*Dave, bake, cake*)

ASSOCIATE LETTERS TO THEIR SOUNDS Write on the board the sentence *Dave can bake a cake for Pat.* Underline the words *can* and *Pat*, and have children read them aloud. Ask how the two words are alike. (*CVC pattern; short a*) Remind children that words with the CVC spelling pattern usually have a short vowel sound. Then circle the words *Dave, bake,* and *cake,* and ask how these words are alike. (*They all have vowel a; they all have e at the end.*) Explain that in words that have a consonant, a vowel, a consonant, and a final *e*, the vowel usually stands for the long vowel sound. Have children repeat the words *Dave, bake,* and *cake* and listen for the long *a* sound.

WORD BLENDING Write *plane* on the board. Model blending the sounds to read *plane:* Slide your hand under the word as you slowly elongate the sounds. Then read the word naturally. Have children practice blending sounds to read aloud these words: *gate, cape,* and *name*.

Practice/Apply

APPLY THE SKILL *Vowel Substitution* Write each of the following words on the board, and have children read it aloud. Make the changes necessary to form the word in parentheses. Have children read each new word.

can (cane)	cap (cape)	plan (plane)	Jan (Jane)	Sam (same)
mad (made)	mat (mate)	hat (hate)	man (mane)	pan (pane)

DICTATION AND WRITING Have children number a sheet of paper 1–8. Dictate the following words, and have children write them. After they write each word, write it on the board so children can proofread their work. On their papers, they should draw a line through a misspelled word and write the correct spelling below it.

1. made	2. same*	3. take*	4. late	*Word appears in
5. game	6. shape*	7. snake	8. grade	"The Earth in Motion."

Dictate the following sentence: *Jane gave her pet snake a name.*

READ LONGER WORDS *Review Compound Words* Write the word *pancake* on the board. Remind children that they can often figure out longer words by looking for smaller words in them. Cover the word *cake,* and have children read *pan.* Follow a similar procedure to have them read *cake.* Model how to blend the two smaller words to read aloud the longer word *pancake.* Follow a similar procedure to have children blend smaller words to read these longer words: *handshake, baseball,* and *nickname.*

REPRODUCIBLE STUDENT ACTIVITY PAGE

INDEPENDENT PRACTICE See the reproducible Student Activity on page 87.

Name _____

The Earth in Motion

Circle and write the word that makes the sentence tell about the picture.

1. Mom said: "Let's get our stuff. I will

   _____ you to the park."

   tackle   tag   (take)

2. Jake got his _____.

   snack   (skates)   sakes

3. Pam packed some sandwiches, milk,

   and _____.

   grab   gave   (grapes)

4. The park had a _____.

   (lake)   last   lamp

5. Jake rested in the _____.

   shack   sad   (shade)

6. Mom _____ some

   (ate)   at   ask

   grapes and a sandwich.

7. Then Mom said, "Now we have to go.

   It is getting _____."

   lake   (late)   lap

Harcourt

Introducing Vocabulary

Apply word identification strategies.

IDENTIFY VOCABULARY WORDS Display the vocabulary words, and ask children to identify the ones they know. Remind children that they can sometimes figure out an unfamiliar word by looking for familiar letter patterns and word parts. Point out the letters *ur* in *turning*. Ask children to use what they know about the sound that *ur* stands for to help them read the word aloud. Then point to each of the other words and read it aloud. Have children read it aloud after you.

VOCABULARY DEFINED
earth planet people live on
hours time periods of 60 minutes
light brightness
night period of darkness between sunset and sunrise
shadow darkness caused by something blocking the light
turning spinning

Check understanding.

Discuss the meanings of the vocabulary words. Then have children write the vocabulary words on a sheet of paper. Have children name the word that answers each of the following questions and circle that word on their papers.

- **What follows day?** *(night)*
- **What is one thing we get from the sun?** *(light)*
- **What are there 24 of in each day?** *(hours)*
- **What is the planet you live on?** *(earth)*
- **What is another word for *spinning*?** *(turning)*
- **What could the shade from a tree be called?** *(shadow)*

REPRODUCIBLE STUDENT ACTIVITY PAGE

INDEPENDENT PRACTICE See the reproducible Student Activity on page 89.

NOTE: The following vocabulary words from "What Makes Day and Night" are reinforced in "The Earth in Motion." If children are unfamiliar with these words, point them out as you encounter them during reading: *motion, toward* (p. 118); *experiment, imagine* (p. 120); *photograph* and *spins* (p. 123).

The Earth in Motion

Read the story.

 We live on the planet **earth**.	 The earth is always **turning**.	 One full turn takes 24 **hours**.
 The sun shines **light** on the earth.	 Part of the earth is in light. The other part is in **shadow**.	 It is **night** on the part of the earth that is in shadow.

Write a story word to complete each sentence.
Choose from the words above in dark type.

1. The _____ is shaped like a ball.

2. The sun's _____ hits part of the earth.

3. The other part of the earth is in _____.

4. It is _____ where the earth is in shadow.

5. The earth is always _____, or spinning.

6. The earth turns once in 24 _____.

Directed Reading

Page 118 Read aloud the title of the story. To demonstrate the meaning of motion, have children make turning motions with their hands. Then ask children what they think this selection will be about. Have children read page 118 to find out why people see the sun in the morning.
Why do people see the sun in the morning? (*The earth is turning them toward the sun.*) INFERENTIAL: CAUSE AND EFFECT

Page 119 Have children read page 119 to find out what happens during the day.
What happens during the day? (Possible response: *The earth keeps turning, and we see the sun.*) INFERENTIAL: INTERPRET STORY EVENTS **What is happening when the light fades?** (Possible response: *It is beginning to get darker.*) INFERENTIAL: UNDERSTAND FIGURA-TIVE LANGUAGE **Now it is night. Why is it dark?** (Possible response: *The earth has turned so you are no longer facing the sun.*) INFERENTIAL: DRAW CONCLUSIONS **What do you think will happen next?** (Possible response: *The earth will keep turning until you are facing the sun again. Then it will be morning.*) CRITICAL: MAIN IDEA

Pages 120–121 Read aloud page 120. Then have children reread it aloud. If possible, have volunteers follow the steps in the experiment as other children are reading.
In the experiment, what is the sun? (*the light*) **What is the earth?** (*the ball*) **What are you?** (*the spot on the ball*) INFERENTIAL: NOTE DETAILS **What do you think you will do next in the experiment?** (Possible response: *Make the earth turn to see what happens to the spot.*) INFERENTIAL: MAKE PREDICTIONS

Page 122 Have children read page 122 to find out about the experiment.
What does the experiment show? (Possible response: *It shows how the earth rotates as it goes around the sun; it shows why we sometimes are in daylight and at other times are in darkness.*) CRITICAL: MAIN IDEA/SYNTHESIZE

Page 123 Have children look at the photograph of the earth on page 123. Ask: **How is the earth like the ball in the experiment?** (Possible response: *It is round; it is turning.*) INFERENTIAL: COMPARE **What can you learn from this selection?** (Possible response: *The earth turns all the time: the sun does not really come up, but the earth turns so you are facing it.*) INFERENTIAL SUMMARIZE

SUMMARIZING THE SELECTION Have children think about what they learned first, next, and last in this selection. Then help them summarize the selection in two or three sentences. INFERENTIAL: SUMMARIZE

Answers to Think About It Questions

Page 124 1. The part of the earth we are on has turned toward the sun. SUMMARY
2. It is evening or night. INTERPRETATION
3. Accept reasonable pictures. TASK

Page 125 For instruction on the Focus Skill: Important Details, see page 125 in *Blue Skies.*

Name _____

The Earth in Motion

Circle the word that best completes each sentence. Write it on the line.

1. The ball is the _____. sun (earth) shadow	**2.** The lamp is the _____. shadow (sun) night
3. The sun shines _____ (light) night shadow on the earth.	**4.** It is _____ hours (day) night where the sun shines on the earth.
5. It is _____ light day (night) where the earth is in shadow.	**6.** It takes 24 _____ days (hours) shadow for the earth to make one full turn.

Write what you learned from this story on the lines below.

Accept reasonable responses.

_____

_____

_____

_____

Harcourt

The Not-So-Boring Night

by Kathryn Corbett   **Use with *Blue Skies*, pages 126–133.**

Preteaching Skills: Long Vowels /ō/o-e; /yōō/u-e

Teach/Model

IDENTIFY THE SOUND Have children repeat the following sentence three times: *I rode a mule that had a cute nose.* Ask them which words in the sentence have the /ō/ sound that they hear in *note.* (*rode, nose*) Then ask which words have the /yōō/ sound that they hear in *use.* (*mule, cute*)

ASSOCIATE LETTERS TO THEIR SOUNDS Write on the board the sentence *I rode a mule that had a cute nose.* Circle the words *rode* and *nose.* Ask how they are alike. (*Both have an* o *and an* e; *both have same vowel sound; the CVCe pattern.*) Underline the letters *o-e* in *rode* and *nose.* Tell children that the letters *o-e* often stand for the long *o* sound they hear in *rode* and *nose.* Have children repeat *rode* and *nose* and listen for the /ō/ sound. Then follow a similar procedure with the letters *u-e* in *mule* and *cute.* Finally, ask how all four words are alike. (*They have the CVCe pattern, which often stands for a long vowel sound.*)

WORD BLENDING Write *hose* on the board. Model blending the sounds to read *hose:* Slide your hand under the word as you slowly elongate the sounds. Then read the word naturally. Have children practice blending sounds to read aloud these words: *rose, hope, fuse,* and *cube.*

Practice/Apply

APPLY THE SKILL *Vowel Substitution* Write each of the following words on the board, and have children read it aloud. Make the changes necessary to form the word in parentheses. Have children read each new word.

pot (pole)   rod (rode)   hop (hope)   not (note)
cub (cube)   mug (mule)   cut (cute)   fuss (fuse)

DICTATION AND WRITING Have children number a sheet of paper 1–7. Dictate the following words, and have children write them. After they have finished, write each word on the board so children can proofread their work. Have them draw a line through a misspelled word and write the correct spelling below it.

1. note   2. cute   3. mule   4. rope   *Word appears in
5. cube   6. nose*   7. poke*   "The Not-So-Boring Night."

READ LONGER WORDS *Review CVC/CVCe* Write the word *notepad* on the board. Remind children that they can often figure out longer words by looking for parts they know. Cover *pad,* and point out the CVCe spelling pattern. Have children use the pattern to help them read the word part. Do the same to have them read *pad.* Point out the CVC pattern. Model how to blend the word parts to read aloud the longer word *notepad.* Do the same to have children blend word parts to read these longer words: *hopeless* and *rosebud.*

REPRODUCIBLE STUDENT ACTIVITY PAGE

INDEPENDENT PRACTICE See the reproducible Student Activity on page 93.

The Not-So-Boring Night

Circle and write the word that makes the sentence tell about the picture.

1. Last summer, Jane rode a

_____ on a camping trip.

       mug   mule   mop

2. Jane, Mom, and Dad rode up a

_____ to a lake.

       slope   cube   stop

3. Jane used a _____

       cute   pot   pole

to catch some fish.

4. Her dad found a red _____.

       run   rose   rock

5. The rose made his _____ itch.

       not   nose   note

6. Mom dug a _____

       hot   hole   hug

and put some stones around it.

7. Jane saw funny shapes in the

_____.

       mule   small   smoke

8. When it got dark, the stars _____

       shone   spoke   song

down on the camp.

Harcourt

Introducing Vocabulary

Apply word identification strategies.

IDENTIFY VOCABULARY WORDS Display the vocabulary words, and ask children to identify the ones they know. Remind children that they can sometimes figure out an unfamiliar word by looking for familiar spelling and letter patterns or smaller word parts. Point out the letters in the CVC pattern in *lunches* and *chickens*. Ask children to use what they know about the CVC spelling pattern and looking for word parts to help them read aloud these words. Point out the letters *ar* and *er* in *farmer* and *or* in *corn*. Have children use what they know about these letter patterns to help them read the words aloud. Then point to *throwing* and read it aloud. Have children read it aloud after you.

Check understanding.

Discuss the meanings of the vocabulary words. Then ask children to write the vocabulary words on a sheet of paper. Have them name the word that completes each sentence and circle that word on their papers.

- **Beth is a ___, or a person who grows things on a farm.** *(farmer)*
- **She grows ___ in her fields.** *(corn)*
- **Beth uses some of the corn to feed her ___.** *(chickens)*
- **Right now, she is ____ corn to the hens.** *(throwing)*
- **Beth sells the ___ that her chickens lay.** *(eggs)*
- **Some people use them for their ___.** *(lunches)*

Children may be unfamiliar with some of the words in the title of the selection that they will read. After distributing the vocabulary page, point to the title, "The Not-So-Boring Night," read it aloud, and have children read it with you.

REPRODUCIBLE STUDENT ACTIVITY PAGE

INDEPENDENT PRACTICE See the reproducible Student Activity on page 95.

NOTE: The following vocabulary words from "The Day Jimmy's Boa Ate the Wash" are reinforced in "The Not-So-Boring Night." If children are unfamiliar with these words, point them out as you encounter them during reading: *boring* (p. 126); *ducked* (p. 128); *supposed*, *sense*, and *never* (p. 129).

Name _____

The Not-So-Boring Night

Read each sentence. Write a word from the box that makes sense in each sentence.

chickens corn eggs farmer lunches throwing

1. Jerome and Duke live next door to a

_____.

2. The farmer has a lot of

_____.

3. He feeds

_____

to the chickens.

4. Sometimes Jerome has fun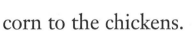

_____

corn to the chickens.

5. One day a week, Jerome gets

_____

from the farmer.

6. Jerome's mom uses the eggs to make

_____.

Harcourt

Directed Reading

Page 126 Read the title aloud. Ask children what they think the title means. Ask: **Where are Rose and Jerome?** (*on the porch of their cabin by the lake*) LITERAL: NOTE DETAILS   **Why does Jerome think it will be a boring night?** (Possible response: *He is playing a fishing game with his younger sister and thinks it is boring.*) INFERENTIAL: UNDERSTAND CHARACTERS' FEELINGS

Page 127 Have children read page 127. Ask: **Why is Jerome glad?** (*His dog, Duke, barked because Duke wanted to go for a walk. If Jerome takes Duke for a walk, he will not have to play with Rose.*) INFERENTIAL: UNDERSTAND CHARACTERS' MOTIVES

Page 128 Read aloud the first sentence of page 128. Ask: **Why does Jerome thank Duke?** (*Duke helped him get out of playing the game with Rose.*) INFERENTIAL: CAUSE AND EFFECT   **What does *doze off* mean?** (*go to sleep*) **How do you know?** (*Rose gets mad when he snores, and you snore when you are asleep.*) INFERENTIAL: USE CONTEXT CLUES   **Who does Jerome see by the dunes?** (*the farmer*) LITERAL: NOTE DETAILS

Page 129 Have children read page 129 to find out what the farmer is doing. Ask: **What is the farmer doing?** (*fishing*) INFERENTIAL: INTERPRET STORY EVENTS   **What is odd about how the farmer is fishing?** (Possible response: *He is throwing back all the fish; he is fishing with a magnet.*) INFERENTIAL: INTERPRET STORY EVENTS

Page 130 Have children read page 130 to find out what is odd about the fish. Ask: **What is odd about the fish?** (*It is red and has a number on it.*) LITERAL: NOTE DETAILS   **Why do you think the farmer is throwing back all the fish?** (Accept reasonable responses.) CRITICAL: UNDERSTAND CHARACTERS' MOTIVES

Page 131 Have children read page 131. Ask: **Why is the farmer throwing the fish back?** (Possible response: *He doesn't like taking fish out of the water; he is playing a game.*) INFERENTIAL: UNDERSTAND CHARACTERS' MOTIVES   **What game is the farmer's game like?** (*Rose's game*) INFERENTIAL: COMPARE   **What do you think is the poke that Jerome feels?** (Accept reasonable responses.) INFERENTIAL: MAKE PREDICTIONS

Page 132 Have children read page 132. Ask: **What is the sharp poke?** (Possible response: *Rose is waking Jerome by poking him.*) INFERENTIAL: DRAW CONCLUSIONS   **How is Rose's fish like the fish in Jerome's dream?** (*Both are red, and both have a number.*) INFERENTIAL: COMPARE   **Why do you think Jerome likes the game at the end?** (Accept reasonable responses.) CRITICAL: EXPRESS AN OPINION

SUMMARIZING THE SELECTION Ask children to think about the order of the events in "The Not-So-Boring Night." Help children summarize the story in a few sentences. INFERENTIAL: SUMMARIZE

Answers to Think About It Questions

Page 133
1. He gets bored, falls asleep, and has a strange dream about a farmer who is fishing with magnets. SUMMARY
2. His dream is not boring; he realizes fishing with magnets can be fun.
   INTERPRETATION
3. Accept reasonable responses. TASK

The Not-So-Boring Night

These events are from "The Not-So-Boring Night." They are out of order. Put a number in front of each one to show the right order.

_____ The farmer was throwing back the fish he got.

_____ Jerome said he liked the fishing game.

_____ Duke and Jerome went for a walk.

_____ Rose woke Jerome up.

Now write each event in the order it happened. Put each one next to an X. Then write other story events on the blank lines.

_____

X _____

X _____

_____

X _____

X _____

Phonics

The Matador and Me

by Kathryn Corbett **Use with *Blue Skies*, pages 134–141.**

Preteaching Skills: Long Vowel /ī/*i-e, ie*

Teach/Model

IDENTIFY THE SOUND Have children repeat the following sentence three times: *Mike flies a kite with a big stripe.* Ask them which words in the sentence have the /ī/ sound they hear in *five.* (*Mike, flies, kite, stripe*)

ASSOCIATE LETTERS TO THEIR SOUND Write on the board the sentence *Mike flies a kite with a big stripe.* Circle the words *with* and *big*, and ask how they are alike. (*short* i, *CVC*) Remind children that when the vowel *i* comes between two or more consonants, it usually stands for the short *i* (/i/) sound.

Circle the words *Mike, kite,* and *stripe*, and ask how they are alike. (*i-e, CVCe*) Underline the letters *i-e* in *Mike, kite,* and *stripe.* Remind children that when a vowel is followed by a consonant and *e*, it usually stands for the long vowel sound. Tell children that the letters *i-e* stand for the /ī/ sound they hear in *Mike, kite,* and *stripe.* Have children repeat the words and listen for the /ī/ sound. Then follow a similar procedure with the letters *ie* in *flies.*

WORD BLENDING Write *dime* on the board. Model blending the sounds to read *dime:* Slide your hand under the word as you slowly elongate the sounds. Then read the word naturally. Have children practice blending sounds to read aloud these words: *bike, pie, tries, wipe.*

Practice/Apply

APPLY THE SKILL *Vowel Substitution* Write each of the following words on the board, and have children read it aloud. Make the changes necessary to form the word in parentheses. Have children read each new word.

rid (ride)	hid (hide)	to (tie)	pins (pies)
dim (dime)	pin (pine)	lit (lie)	flips (flies)

DICTATION AND WRITING Have children number a sheet of paper 1–8. Write the word *time* on the board, and tell children that in the words you say, /ī/ will be spelled *i-e.* Dictate the words, and have children write them. After they have finished, write each word on the board so children can proofread their work. Have them draw a line through a misspelled word and write the correct spelling above it.

1. ride	2. nine	3. wide	4. kite	*Word appears in
5. pride	6. mine*	7. size*	8. pile	"The Matador and Me."*

Tell children that in the following sentence, /ī/ will be spelled *ie.* Dictate the sentence: *He tries to get the pie.*

REPRODUCIBLE STUDENT ACTIVITY PAGE
....
INDEPENDENT PRACTICE See the reproducible Student Activity on page 99.

READ LONGER WORDS *Review Compound Words* Write the word *sunshine* on the board. Remind children that they can often figure out longer words by looking for smaller words in them. Cover *shine*, and have children read the smaller word. Follow a similar procedure to have them read the smaller word *shine.* Model how to blend the two smaller words to read aloud the longer word *sunshine.* Have children blend smaller words to read these longer words: *pinstripe* and *butterflies.*

The Matador and Me

Write the word that best completes each sentence.

hike	kite	pies	stripes	tie	shines	rides

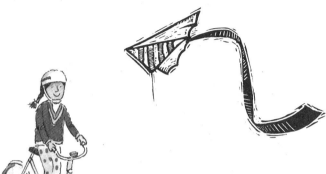

1. Todd likes to play with his
_____.

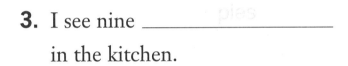

2. Jane _____
her bike to the lake.

3. I see nine _____
in the kitchen.

4. Tim and Mike went for a
_____ up a hill.

5. Dom stops to _____
his laces well.

6. Dave wore a shirt with black
_____.

7. The sun _____
on the vines.

Harcourt

Introducing Vocabulary

Apply word identification strategies.

IDENTIFY VOCABULARY WORDS Display the vocabulary words, and ask children to identify the ones they know. Remind children that they can sometimes figure out an unfamiliar word by thinking about the sounds that letters stand for. Then point to and read each vocabulary word aloud. Have children read it aloud after you.

Check understanding.

Discuss the meanings of the vocabulary words. Then ask children to write the vocabulary words on a sheet of paper. Have them name the word that answers each of the following questions and circle that word on their papers.

- **What word best completes this sentence?** *I play soccer ___ of basketball.* (*instead*)
- **Who are the people who ride horses on cattle drives?** (*cowboys*)
- **What word means "mom and dad"?** (*parents*)
- **What word names something that goes on tracks?** (*train*)
- **Who is your mom's sister?** (*aunt*)
- **What do people wear?** (*clothes*)

Children may be unfamiliar with some of the words in the title of the selection that they will read. After distributing the vocabulary page, point to the title, "The Matador and Me," read it aloud, and have children read it with you.

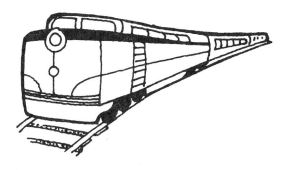

REPRODUCIBLE STUDENT ACTIVITY PAGE

INDEPENDENT PRACTICE See the reproducible Student Activity on page 101.

NOTE: The following vocabulary words from "How I Spent My Summer Vacation" are reinforced in "The Matador and Me." If children are unfamiliar with these words, point them out as you encounter them during reading: *matador, vacation, plain, imagination, captured, relax,* and *manners* (all on p. 134).

Read the letter. Then write a letter from Jane to Aunt Clementine. Use all the words in dark type in your answers.

Dear Jane,

I will meet your **train** next week at five o'clock. We will have fun watching **cowboys** rope and ride. We can camp out under the stars or sleep in a tent **instead**.

Be sure to pack lots of **clothes**. Give your **parents** a hug from me.

Love,
Aunt Clementine

_____ ,

Dear _____

_____

_____

_____

_____

_____

_____

_____

Love,
Jane

Directed Reading

NOTE: Read the entire story (pp. 134–139) aloud to children before they read it silently. Be sure to emphasize the rhyme and meter of the story.

Page 134　Read aloud the title to children. Ask what a matador is. (*a bullfighter*) Have children read page 134. Ask: **Where does the girl go for vacation?** (*to visit her Aunt Clementine*) LITERAL: NOTE DETAILS　**What does it mean to "work one's imagination overtime"?** (Accept reasonable responses, which might include being very creative or making things up a lot.) INFERENTIAL: SPECULATE

Page 135　Have children read page 135 to find out about Aunt Clementine. **How is Aunt Clementine different from the girl's parents?** (Possible response: *The girl's parents tell her to use good manners and to behave. Aunt Clementine thinks rules are for parents and school.*) INFERENTIAL: COMPARE AND CONTRAST　**What is the only thing missing when the girl visits her aunt?** (*someone to play games with; someone her age*) INFERENTIAL: UNDERSTAND AUTHOR'S USE OF LANGUAGE　**What do you think the surprise will be?** (Possible response: *a playmate*) INFERENTIAL: MAKE PREDICTIONS

Page 136　Have children read page 136. Ask: **What is the surprise?** (*a big kid that is dressed like a matador*) INFERENTIAL: CONFIRM PREDICTIONS

Page 137　Read aloud the first sentence of page 137, and discuss the meaning of the word *glum*. **Why is the boy glum?** (*He couldn't get the bulls to do what they were supposed to do.*) INFERENTIAL: UNDERSTAND CHARACTERS' FEELINGS　**What does the girl pretend to be?** (*a bull*) INFERENTIAL: DRAW CONCLUSIONS　**What do you think will happen next?** (Accept reasonable responses.) INFERENTIAL: MAKE PREDICTIONS

Page 138　Have children read page 138 to find out what happens to the boy.　**What happens to the boy?** (*He falls down.*) LITERAL: NOTE DETAILS　**How does the boy feel?** (Possible response: *angry, frustrated, and sad*) INFERENTIAL: UNDERSTAND CHARACTERS' EMOTIONS　**What do you think the boy will decide about being a matador?** (Accept reasonable responses.) INFERENTIAL: MAKE PREDICTIONS

Page 139　Have children read page 139. Ask: **What does the boy decide to do?** (Possible response: *He decides not to be a matador but to be a farmer instead.*) INFERENTIAL: INTERPRET STORY EVENTS　**How does the girl help?** (Possible response: *She names other things he can do.*) INFERENTIAL: SUMMARIZE　**Do you think the girl's story is true?** (Accept reasonable responses.) CRITICAL: EXPRESS OPINIONS

SUMMARIZING THE SELECTION Have children think about what happened first, next, and last in the story. Then help them summarize the selection in three sentences. INFERENTIAL: SUMMARIZE

Answers to Think About It Questions

Page 140
1. The girl goes to visit her aunt. She meets a new pal and helps him decide not to be a matador. SUMMARY
2. No, he has not, because he is not very good at being a matador. He is also very young to be a matador. INTERPRETATION
3. Accept reasonable responses. TASK

Page 141　For instruction on the Focus Skill: Context Clues for Word Meaning, see page 141 in *Blue Skies.*

Name _____

Complete the puzzle using the words in the box. The answer for 2 Down has been done for you.

| parents   cowboys   aunt   train   instead   clothes |

Across

3. Matadors wear _____ that glitter and shine.

5. The girl's _____ think she has a big imagination.

7. The girl takes a _____ out west.

Down

1. The _____ howled when the matador fell down.

2. The big kid was dressed like a _____.

4. The matador wants to be a farmer _____.

6. The girl's _____ has a ranch on the plains.

Crossword grid:
2 Down: m a t a d o r
5 Across: p a r e n t s
7 Across: t r a i n

Write about your favorite part of the story. Use as many words from the box as you can.

_____

_____

_____

_____

Harcourt

Mr. Whiskers

by Meish Goldish   **Use with *Blue Skies*, pages 142–149.**

Preteaching Skills: Long Vowel /ē/ee, ea

Teach/Model

IDENTIFY THE SOUND Have children repeat the following sentence three times: *Ben feeds beans and beets to Jean and Ted.* Ask children which words in the sentence have the /ē/ sound they hear in *speak.* (*feeds, beans, beets, Jean*)

ASSOCIATE LETTERS TO THEIR SOUND Write on the board the sentence *Ben feeds beans and beets to Jean and Ted.* Circle the words *Ben* and *Ted*, and ask how they are alike. (*short* e; *CVC*) Remind children that when the vowel *e* comes between two consonants, it usually stands for the short *e* sound.

Circle the words *feeds* and *beets*, and ask how they are alike. (*ee*) Underline the letters *ee* in *feeds* and *beets.* Explain that when two vowels come together in a word, they often stand for the long vowel sound of the first vowel. Tell children that the letters *ee* often stand for the /ē/ sound they hear in *feeds* and *beets.* Have children repeat the words and listen for the /ē/ sound. Then follow a similar procedure with the letters *ea* in *beans* and *Jean.*

WORD BLENDING Write *green* on the board. Model blending the sounds to read *green:* Slide your hand under the word as you slowly elongate the sounds. Then read the word naturally. Have children practice blending sounds to read aloud these words: *tree, read, beak.*

Practice/Apply

APPLY THE SKILL *Vowel Substitution* Write each of the following words on the board, and have children read it aloud. Make the changes necessary to form each word in parentheses. Have children read each new word.

fed (feed)	met (meet)	bed (bead)	set (seat)
step (steep)	sped (speed)	net (neat)	led (lead)

DICTATION AND WRITING Have children number a sheet of paper 1–8. Write *beet* on the board and tell children that in the words you say, the long *e* sound is spelled *ee* as in *beet.* Dictate the words, and have children write them. After they have finished, write each word on the board so children can proofread their work. Have them draw a line through a misspelled word and write the correct spelling above it.

1. need*	2. deep*	3. sleep	4. street	*Word appears in
5. meet*	6. sheet	7. see*	8. cheeks*	"Mr. Whiskers."

Tell children that in the following sentence, /ē/ will be spelled *ea.* Dictate the sentence: *I dream that seals in the sea swim to the beach.*

READ LONGER WORDS *Review Compound Words* Display the word *beanbag.* Remind children that they can often figure out longer words by looking for smaller words in them. Cover *bag*, and have children read the smaller word that is left. Do the same to have them read *bag.* Model how to blend the smaller words to read aloud the longer word *beanbag.* Have children blend smaller words to read these words: *dreamland, teatime, teammate.*

REPRODUCIBLE STUDENT ACTIVITY PAGE
....
INDEPENDENT PRACTICE See the reproducible Student Activity on page 105.

Name _____

Mr. Whiskers

Fill in the oval in front of the sentence that best tells about the picture.

1 ◯ The cat is sleeping.
   ◯ Chen is eating beets.
   ◯ Chen is feeding her pet.

2 ◯ Fred and Kent have no sheets.
   ◯ I see three beds.
   ◯ Fred is dreaming of sheep.

3 ◯ Tom is sleeping on the beach.
   ◯ A seal is swimming in the deep sea.
   ◯ Meg has sneakers on her feet.

4 ◯ The sheep are near a tree.
   ◯ I see three sheep and a bee.
   ◯ The sheep are eating beans.

5 ◯ Ron is feeding the birds.
   ◯ Three cats are in a tree.
   ◯ Three birds in a tree want to eat.

6 ◯ I see bees in that tree.
   ◯ There is one leaf left on that tree.
   ◯ The leaf fell in the street.

Harcourt

Introducing Vocabulary

Apply word identification strategies.

IDENTIFY VOCABULARY WORDS Display the vocabulary words, and ask children to try to identify the ones they know. Remind children that they can sometimes figure out an unfamiliar word by looking for familiar spelling or letter patterns. Point out the CVC(C) pattern in *lost* and *pond*. Ask children to use what they know about CVC to read these words aloud. Follow a similar procedure with the CVC*e* pattern in the word *whales* and the CVVC pattern in *beach*. Then read *dear* and *water* aloud. Have children read each word aloud after you.

Check understanding.

Discuss the meanings of the vocabulary words. Then have children write the vocabulary words on a sheet of paper. Ask children to name the word that completes each of the following sentences and to circle that word on their papers.

- **If a dog can't find its way home, it is ___.** *(lost)*
- **We make sandcastles on the ___.** *(beach)*
- **Do you swim in ocean ___?** *(water)*
- **A ___ is a small lake.** *(pond)*
- **I saw some ___ swimming in the ocean.** *(whales)*
- **Sometimes my mom calls me "___."** *(dear)*

Children may be unfamiliar with words in the title of the selection that they will read. After distributing the vocabulary page, point to the title, "Mr. Whiskers," read it aloud, and have children read it with you.

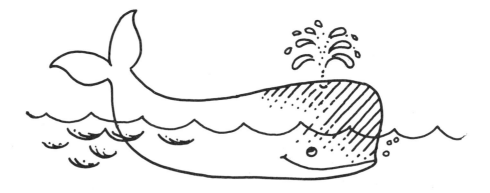

REPRODUCIBLE STUDENT ACTIVITY PAGE

INDEPENDENT PRACTICE See the reproducible Student Activity on page 107.

NOTE: The following vocabulary words from "Dear Mr. Blueberry" are reinforced in "Mr. Whiskers." If children are unfamiliar with these words, point them out as you encounter them during reading: *ocean, information* (p. 142); *forcibly* (p. 144); *details* and *disappoints* (p. 148).

Name _____

Mr. Whiskers

Read the ad.

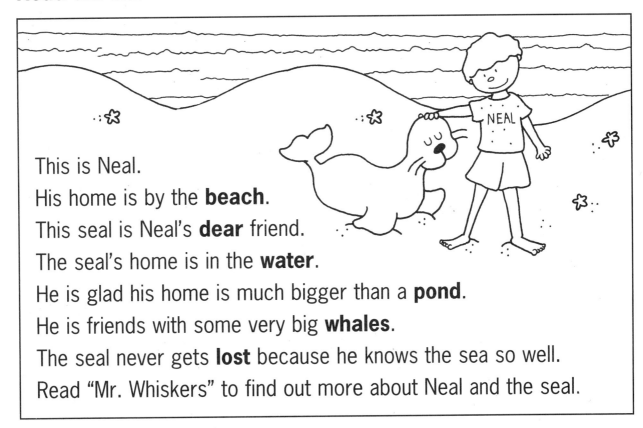

This is Neal.
His home is by the **beach**.
This seal is Neal's **dear** friend.
The seal's home is in the **water**.
He is glad his home is much bigger than a **pond**.
He is friends with some very big **whales**.
The seal never gets **lost** because he knows the sea so well.
Read "Mr. Whiskers" to find out more about Neal and the seal.

Write a word from the ad to complete each sentence. Choose from the words in dark type.

1. Neal has a _____dear_____ friend who is a seal.

2. You can swim in _____water_____, but not on land.

3. The seal never gets _____lost_____ in the sea.

4. Neal's home is by the _____beach_____.

5. Seals are small, but _____whales_____ are big.

6. A _____pond_____ is like a little lake.

Harcourt

Directed Reading

Page 142 Read aloud the title of the story. Ask children who they think Mr. Whiskers is. Then have them read page 142 to find out. **Who is Mr. Whiskers? Where does Mr. Whiskers live?** (*Mr. Whiskers is a seal. He lives in the sea.*) LITERAL: NOTE DETAILS **Who is Neal? Where does Neal live?** (*Neal is the boy telling the story. He lives in a home on the beach.*) LITERAL: NOTE DETAILS **What does Neal learn from Mr. Whiskers?** (*He learns about other animals that live in the ocean.*) INFERENTIAL: INTERPRET STORY EVENTS

Page 143 Have children read page 143 to find out why Mr. Whiskers likes living in the ocean. **Why does Mr. Whiskers like living in the ocean?** (Possible response: *It is very big and a lot of animals live in it.*) INFERENTIAL: CAUSE AND EFFECT

Page 144 Have children read page 144 to find out more about seals. **What are three things you read about seals?** (Possible response: *Seals are good swimmers; they use their flippers to help them swim fast; they swim far distances.*) INFERENTIAL: SUMMARIZE

Page 145 Ask children to read page 145 to find out about a swimming contest. **Who is having a swimming contest?** (*all the seals*) INFERENTIAL: DRAW CONCLUSIONS **Who won the swimming contest?** (*Mr. Whiskers*) LITERAL: NOTE DETAILS

Page 146 Have children read page 146 to find out how Mr. Whiskers got his name. **How did Mr. Whiskers get his name?** (*He has long whiskers.*) INFERENTIAL: DRAW CONCLUSIONS **How do whiskers help seals?** (*They help seals feel around in the water; they help seals find fish to eat.*) LITERAL: NOTE DETAILS

Page 147 Have children read page 147 to find out whether seals make good pets. **Do seals make good pets? Why?** (Possible response: *No, because they don't walk well on land; they are wild animals.*) INFERENTIAL: DRAW CONCLUSIONS **Why does Neal want to be a seal?** (Possible response: *He wouldn't have to take baths because he would always be clean.*) INFERENTIAL: UNDERSTAND CHARACTERS' MOTIVATIONS **Do you think Neal really wants to be a seal?** (Answers will vary.) CRITICAL: SPECULATE

Page 148 Have children read page 148 to find out what Neal's parents think about Mr. Whiskers. **Have Neal's parents ever seen Mr. Whiskers?** (*no*) LITERAL: NOTE DETAILS **What do Neal's parents think about Mr. Whiskers?** (*They think he is not real.*) INFERENTIAL: DRAW CONCLUSIONS **Do you think Mr. Whiskers is real? Why or why not?** (Answers will vary.) CRITICAL: EXPRESS PERSONAL OPINIONS

SUMMARIZING THE SELECTION Ask children to think about what Neal learns about seals. Then help children use this information to summarize the story. INFERENTIAL: SUMMARIZE

Answers to Think About It Questions

Possible responses for items 1–3 are shown below.

Page 149
1. Seals have whiskers that they use to help them feel for food in the water. Seals swim fast and far. SUMMARY
2. They do not believe that a seal would come to the beach each weekend and speak to their son. INTERPRETATION
3. Accept reasonable pictures. TASK

Name _____

Mr. Whiskers

Neal tells a lot about Mr. Whiskers. Write *first*, *next*, or *last* under each picture to show when Neal tells about each thing.

_____   _____   _____

Complete each sentence so it tells about the story. Choose from the words in dark type.

1. Neal and Mr. Whiskers are _____ friends.

sad   sorry   dear

2. Sometimes Mr. Whiskers meets Neal at

the _____.

pond   beach   deck

3. Mr. Whiskers has made friends with big

_____.

whales   cats   shells

4. Mr. Whiskers lives in the _____.

water   forest   barn

5. Mr. Whiskers swims fast and far without getting

_____.

home   hungry   lost

Harcourt

Story Comprehension • Grade 2   **109**

If a Dinosaur Went to the Vet

by Cheyenne Cisco   Use with *Blue Skies*, pages 150–157.

Preteaching Skills: Long Vowel /ā/ai, ay

Teach/Model

IDENTIFY THE SOUND Have children repeat the following sentence three times: *Jan and Jane play with pails in the rain all day.* Ask children to name the words from the sentence that have the /ā/ sound they hear in *may.* (*Jane, play, pails, rain, day*)

ASSOCIATE LETTERS TO THEIR SOUNDS On the board, write the sentence *Jan and Jane play with pails in the rain all day.* Circle the words *Jan* and *and.* Ask children to read aloud the words and to tell how they are alike. (*Both have the /a/, or short a, sound.*) Then circle the word *Jane.* Remind children about the CVC*e* spelling pattern, and then have them read aloud the word and identify the vowel sound. (*/ā/ or long a*) Circle *play* and *day,* and ask how these two words are like *Jane.* (*long a sound*) Underline the letters *ay* in *play* and *day.* Tell children that the letters *ay* usually stand for the /ā/ sound. Then do the same with the letters *ai* in *pails* and *rain.*

WORD BLENDING Write *train* on the board. Model blending the sounds to read *train:* Slide your hand under the word as you slowly elongate the sounds. Then read the word naturally. Have children practice blending sounds to read aloud these words: *chain, sail, hay, clay.*

Practice/Apply

APPLY THE SKILL *Vowel Substitution* Write each of the following words on the board, and have children read it aloud. Make the changes necessary to form the word in parentheses. Have children read each new word.

see (say)   we (way)   ran (rain)   pal (pail)

DICTATION AND WRITING Have children number a sheet of paper 1–8. Write *main* on the board and tell children that in the words you say, the long *a* sound is spelled *ai* as in *main.* Dictate the words and have children write them. After they write each word, write it on the board so children can proofread their work. Have them draw a line through any misspelled words and write the correct spelling above them.

1. faint*	2. wait*	3. sprain*	4. rain*	*Word appears in "If a
5. tail*	6. pain*	7. train	8. snail	Dinosaur Went to the Vet."*

Then dictate the following sentence: *May we stay and play in the hay today?*

READ LONGER WORDS Write the word *crayon* on the board. Remind children to figure out longer words by looking for smaller parts. Cover the letters *on,* and have children read the word part that is left. Do the same to have them read the word part *on.* Model how to blend the word parts to read aloud the longer word *crayon.* Have children blend word parts to read these longer words: *raining, daytime, haystack.*

REPRODUCIBLE STUDENT ACTIVITY PAGE

INDEPENDENT PRACTICE See the reproducible Student Activity on page 111.

If a Dinosaur Went to the Vet

Read the story, and circle all the words with *ai* or *ay*.

One day Gail, her dad, and her dog Brain went for a hike. Brain started to bark. "Brain, are you barking at the snail on that log?" Gail asked. Brain barked some more. "Are you barking at the jay in that

tree?" she asked. Brain barked some more. "Are you barking at the ball on the trail?" Brain wagged his tail. Gail said, "I see! You want to play with that ball. Let's go!"

Choose from the words you circled to finish each sentence.

1. _____ is the name of Gail's dog.

2. Gail asks Brain if he is barking at a _____ on a log.

3. Gail asks Brain if he is barking at a _____ in a tree.

4. Brain is barking at a ball on the _____.

5. Gail knows this after Brain wags his _____.

6. Gail knows Brain wants to _____ with the ball.

Introducing Vocabulary

IDENTIFY VOCABULARY WORDS Display the vocabulary words, and ask children to identify the ones they know. Remind children that they can sometimes figure out an unfamiliar word by thinking about spelling patterns, letter patterns, and word parts. Point out the CVC*e* pattern in the second part of *alive*. Have children use this pattern to help them read the word part. Then ask children to read the word aloud. Follow a similar procedure with the *er* in *herd* and the CVC pattern and the *er* in the words parts in *different*. Then point to and read each of the other vocabulary words aloud. (*dinosaur, imagine, probably*) Have children read them aloud after you.

VOCABULARY DEFINED
alive living
different not the same
dinosaur a kind of reptile that lived and died long ago
herd a large group of animals
imagine to guess; to suppose
probably very likely

Check understanding.

Discuss the meanings of the vocabulary words. Then ask children to write the vocabulary words on a sheet of paper. Have them name the word that answers each of the following questions and circle that word on their papers.

What word . . .

- means "not the same"? *(different)*
- names an animal that lived long ago and could be as tall as a building? *(dinosaur)*
- means "living," or "not dead"? *(alive)*
- means "most likely"? *(probably)*
- names a large group of horses? *(herd)*
- could complete this sentence: *Can you ___ why dinosaurs became extinct? (imagine)*

Children may be unfamiliar with some of the words in the title of the selection that they will read. After distributing the vocabulary page, point to the title, "If a Dinosaur Went to the Vet," read it aloud, and have children read it with you.

NOTE: The following vocabulary words from "It's Probably Good Dinosaurs Are Extinct" are reinforced in "If a Dinosaur Went to the Vet." If children are unfamiliar with these words, point them out as you encounter them during reading: *roamed* (p. 150); *veterinarian* (p. 151); *halt* (p. 151); *extinct* (p. 151); *courage* (p. 152).

REPRODUCIBLE STUDENT ACTIVITY PAGE

INDEPENDENT PRACTICE See the reproducible Student Activity on page 113.

If a Dinosaur Went to the Vet

Read each sentence. Write the word from the box that makes sense in the sentence.

probably	alive	different	herd	dinosaur	imagine

You are _____ from a cat or a dog.

I think you are a _____!

I never did _____ I would see an animal as big as you!

I am _____ the biggest animal you have ever helped.

I didn't think animals like you were still _____.

Oh, yes. I am part of a big _____.

Harcourt

Directed Reading

Pages 150–151 Read aloud the title of the story and the words on the sign. (**Dr. Gail, Veterinarian**) Ask children what a veterinarian, or vet, does. (*treats sick animals*) Then have children read page 150 to find out what animal comes to see Dr. Gail. **What animal comes to see Dr. Gail?** (*a dinosaur*) LITERAL: NOTE DETAILS **What animals usually come to see Dr. Gail?** (*stray cats and dogs*) INFERENTIAL: DRAW CONCLUSIONS **What is a stray?** (*a cat or a dog that is lost or has no home*) INFERENTIAL: PRIOR KNOWLEDGE Have children read page 151 to find out why the dinosaur, Fay, comes to see Dr. Gail. **Why does Fay come to see Dr. Gail?** (*She has a pain; she may faint.*) INFERENTIAL: DRAW CONCLUSIONS **Why must Dr. Gail look way, way up?** (*Fay is very big.*) INFERENTIAL: DRAW CONCLUSIONS **Do you think Dr. Gail can help Fay?** (Accept reasonable responses.) INFERENTIAL: MAKE PREDICTIONS

Page 152 Have children read page 152 to find out why Fay feels faint. **Why does Fay feel faint?** (*from the pain in her tail*) LITERAL: CAUSE AND EFFECT **What does *have courage* mean?** (*be strong; don't be scared*) INFERENTIAL: USE CONTEXT CLUES **What do you think Dr. Gail will see on Fay's tail?** (Accept reasonable responses.) INFERENTIAL: MAKE PREDICTIONS

Page 153 Have children read page 153 to find out is wrong with Fay's tail and how it got hurt. **What is wrong with Fay's tail?** (*It's probably sprained.*) INFERENTIAL: DRAW CONCLUSIONS **How did Fay's tail get hurt?** (*She probably sprained it when she hit the gate.*) INFERENTIAL: DRAW CONCLUSIONS **Why do you think Dr. Gail says, "Ow! Now I've got a sprain"?** (Possible response: *Fay's tail knocks Dr. Gail down, and Dr. Gail gets hurt.*) INFERENTIAL: CAUSE AND EFFECT

Page 154 Have children read page 154 to find out what directions Dr. Gail gives Fay. **What directions does Dr. Gail give Fay?** (*Rub medicine on her tail; stay out of the rain; don't wag your tail.*) INFERENTIAL: FOLLOW DIRECTIONS **Why does Fay think Dr. Gail is a good vet?** (Possible response: *Dr. Gail made her tail feel better.*) INFERENTIAL: UNDERSTAND CHARACTERS' FEELINGS

Page 155 Have children read page 155 to find out what is the same for Dr. Gail and what is different. **What is the same for Dr. Gail? What is different?** (*She stills plays vet; and she still sees strays. Now, though, Dr. Gail only sees cats and dogs.*) INFERENTIAL: CAUSE AND EFFECT

SUMMARIZING THE SELECTION Have children make stick puppets of Dr. Gail and Fay the dinosaur. Ask them to use the puppets to retell the story. Then help them summarize the story. INFERENTIAL: SUMMARIZE

Answers to Think About It Questions

Page 156
1. She gives Fay something to rub on her tail. Then she tells Fay to stay out of the rain and to stop wagging her tail. SUMMARY
2. No, she doesn't want to treat dinosaurs. She adds the words *Just Cats and Dogs* to her sign. INTERPRETATION
3. Accept reasonable responses, which should reflect an understanding of the story. WRITE A SPEECH

Page 157 For instruction on the Focus Skill: Reality and Fantasy, see page 157 in *Blue Skies*.

Name _____

REPRODUCIBLE
STUDENT
ACTIVITY PAGE

If a Dinosaur Went to the Vet

Complete the flowchart with words from the box to tell what happened in "If a Dinosaur Went to the Vet."

different	probably	dinosaur	imagine	alive	herd

Fay was __different__ from a stray cat or dog.

Fay was a stray __dinosaur__!

Dr. Gail did not think that dinosaurs were __alive__ anymore.

Dr. Gail didn't __imagine__ she would help an animal as big as Fay.

Fay said the pain was __probably__ in her tail.

Fay said she would tell the __herd__ about Dr. Gail.

Answer these questions to tell about the rest of the story.

1. How does Dr. Gail get a sprain? Fay's tail knocks her down.

2. How does Dr. Gail help Fay? She gives Fay medicine to rub on her tail and tells Fay how to take care of it.

Selection Comprehension• Grade 2 **115**

Sounds All Around

by Susan M. Fischer   **Use with _Blue Skies_, pages 158–165.**

Preteaching Skills: Vowel Variants /o͞o/u-e, ue, ui

Teach/Model

IDENTIFY THE SOUND Have children repeat the following sentence three times: _Sue eats fruit in June._ Ask children to name the words in the sentence that have the /o͞o/ sound. (_Sue, fruit, June_)

ASSOCIATE LETTERS TO THEIR SOUNDS Write on the board the sentence _Sue eats fruit in June._ Circle the words _Sue, fruit,_ and _June._ Ask children to tell how the words are alike. (_All have the /o͞o/ sound._) Then underline the letters _ue_ in _Sue, ui_ in _fruit,_ and _u-e_ in _June._ Tell children that the letters _ue, ui,_ and _u-e_ can all stand for the /o͞o/ sound they hear in _Sue, fruit,_ and _June._ Have children repeat each word and listen for the /o͞o/ sound.

WORD BLENDING Write _blue_ on the board. Model blending the sounds to read _blue:_ Slide your hand under the word as you slowly elongate the sounds. Then read the word naturally. Have children practice blending sounds to read aloud these words: _true, flute, suit,_ and _tune._

Practice/Apply

APPLY THE SKILL _Vowel Substitution_ Write each of the following words on the board, and have children read it aloud. Make the changes necessary to form the word in parentheses. Have children read each new word.

so (Sue)	sit (suit)	role (rule)	Jane (June)
clay (clue)	fret (fruit)	dud (dude)	tub (tube)

DICTATION AND WRITING Have children number a sheet of paper 1–8. Write the letters _u-e_ on the board and tell children that in the words you say, the /o͞o/ sound is spelled _u-e._ Dictate the words and have children write them. After they write each word, display it on the board so children can proofread their work. Have them draw a line through any misspelled words and write the correct spelling below them.

1. duke	2. plume	3. tube	4. dune	_*Word appears in_
5. June	6. tune*	7. rule	8. flute*	_"Sounds All Around."_

Tell children that in the following sentence, /o͞o/ will be spelled _ue._ Then dictate the sentence: _Sue has a true clue that is blue._

READ LONGER WORDS _Review Compound Words_ Write the word _fruitcake_ on the board. Remind children that they can often figure out longer words by looking for smaller words in it. Cover the word _cake,_ and have children read the remaining word. Follow a similar procedure to have them read the word _cake._ Model how to blend the two smaller words to read aloud the longer word _fruitcake._ Have children do the same to blend the smaller words to read these longer words: _suitcase_ and _bluebird._

REPRODUCIBLE STUDENT ACTIVITY PAGE
....
INDEPENDENT PRACTICE See the reproducible Student Activity on page 117.

Name _____

Sounds All Around

Write the word from the box that best completes each sentence.

bluebird	flute	glue	fruit	suit	ruler

1. June is playing a tune on her _____.

2. I see _____ in that basket.

3. The _____ sings for Sue.

4. Sam has on a black _____.

5. The _____ helps Marta draw a line.

6. Gunther uses _____ to make a model plane.

Harcourt

Introducing Vocabulary

IDENTIFY VOCABULARY WORDS Display the vocabulary words, and ask children to identify the ones they know. Remind children that they can sometimes figure out an unfamiliar word by thinking about spelling patterns, letter patterns, and word parts. Point out the *oo* in *cool*. Have children use what they have learned about these letters to help them read the word. Then ask children to read the word aloud. Follow a similar procedure with the *cr* and *ow* in *crowd*, the *ai* in *rain*, and the CVC*e* pattern and the smaller words in *sidewalk*. Then point to and read each of the other vocabulary words aloud. (*chalk, drawings*) Have children read them aloud after you.

VOCABULARY DEFINED
chalk something used for drawing or writing on the chalkboard
cool good or great
crowd a lot of people
drawings pictures
rain to fall from the clouds as in water droplets; the water droplets that fall from the sky
sidewalk a path for walking along the side of a street

Check understanding.

Discuss the meanings of the vocabulary words. Then ask children to write the vocabulary words on a sheet of paper. Have them name the word that answers each of the following questions and circle that word on their papers.

- **If you think something is special, what word might you use to describe it?** (*cool*)
- **Where do you sometimes run?** (*sidewalk*)
- **What word best completes this sentence:** *Was there a big ___ at the game?* (*crowd*)
- **What would you use to write on the board?** (*chalk*)
- **What might fall from the sky and get you wet?** (*rain*)
- **What can you make with pencils or crayons?** (*drawings*)

Children may be unfamiliar with some of the words in the title of the selection that they will read. After distributing the vocabulary page, point to the title, "Sounds All Around," read it aloud, and have children read it with you.

REPRODUCIBLE STUDENT ACTIVITY PAGE

INDEPENDENT PRACTICE See the reproducible Student Activity on page 119.

NOTE: The following vocabulary words from "Cool Ali" are reinforced in "Sounds All Around." If children are unfamiliar with these words, point them out as you encounter them during reading: *notice* (p. 158); *haze* (p. 160); *pale* (p. 160); *fussed* (p. 160); *admired* (p. 161); and *mimicked* (p. 163).

Name _____

Sounds All Around

Read the ad.

Jules likes to watch Mr. Jones make **drawings** with **chalk**. Sue likes to play **cool** tunes on her flute. Jules likes the sound of **rain** falling on the **sidewalk**. Jules is sad because Mrs. Lee is not in the **crowd**. She is sick. What can Jules do to help Mrs. Lee? Read "Sounds All Around" and find out.

Write a word from the ad to complete each sentence. Choose from the words in dark type.

1. Mr. Jones likes to make _____drawings_____.

2. He uses _____chalk_____ when he draws.

3. Sue plays _____cool_____ tunes.

4. Suddenly it starts to _____rain_____.

5. The rain makes the _____sidewalk_____ wet.

6. Mrs. Lee is not in the _____crowd_____.

Harcourt

Directed Reading

Page 158 Read aloud the title of the story. Ask children what they might hear all around. Then have children read page 158 to see if Jules, the boy in the story, hears some sounds. **Does Jules hear sounds as he walks home?** (*not yet*) INFERENTIAL: INTERPRET STORY EVENTS **What does Jules notice?** (*Mrs. Lee is not home.*) LITERAL: NOTE DETAILS **Why is Jules sad?** (Possible response: *He misses Mrs. Lee.*) INFERENTIAL: IDENTIFY CHARACTERS' FEELINGS

Page 159 Have children read to find out whether Jules hears some sounds. **Does Jules hear some sounds?** (*yes*) **What does he hear?** (*Mr. Jones's chalk on the sidewalk; children playing; Mrs. Peck selling fruit; Sue's tune on her flute; a dump truck; rain*) INFERENTIAL: INTERPRET STORY EVENTS **What do you think Jules's plan is?** (Accept reasonable responses.) INFERENTIAL: MAKE PREDICTIONS

Page 160 Have children read page 160 to find out what Jules does the next day. **What does Jules do the next morning?** (*He visits Mrs. Lee in the hospital.*) LITERAL: NOTE DETAILS **What do you think is in the bag?** (Accept reasonable responses.) INFERENTIAL: MAKE PREDICTIONS

Page 161 Have children read page 161 to find out what is in Jules's bag. **What is in Jules's bag?** (*fruit from Mrs. Peck, drawings from the children, and chalk from Mr. Jones*) LITERAL: NOTE DETAILS **What do you think the coolest present of all will be?** (Accept reasonable responses, but encourage children to think about the title as they answer.) INFERENTIAL: MAKE PREDICTIONS

Pages 162–163 Have children read page 162 to find out about the coolest present of all. **What is the coolest present of all?** (*a tape-recording of sounds from the neighborhood*) INFERENTIAL: CONFIRM PREDICTIONS **What are the sounds on the tape?** (*fruit dropping into a bag; kids jumping rope; a truck; Sue's tune*) INFERENTIAL: SUMMARIZE **Does Mrs. Lee like the tape? How do you know?** (*Yes. She claps and says, "Thank you, Jules!"*) INFERENTIAL: UNDERSTAND CHARACTERS' FEELINGS **Why might Mrs. Lee like the tape?** (Possible response: *It makes her feel as if she is home.*) CRITICAL: IDENTIFY WITH CHARACTERS

Page 164 Read aloud the first sentence on page 164. Then have children read page 164 to find out about the last sound on the tape. **What is the last sound on the tape?** (*the sound of rain*) INFERENTIAL: DRAW CONCLUSIONS **Why do you think Mrs. Lee draws a rainbow?** (Accept reasonable responses.) INFERENTIAL: SPECULATE **Does Jules's plan work?** (*Yes. He plans to cheer up Mrs. Lee, and he does.*) INFERENTIAL: DRAW CONCLUSIONS

SUMMARIZING THE SELECTION Have children think about what happens first, next, and last. Then help them summarize the story in three sentences. INFERENTIAL: SUMMARIZE

Answers to Think About It Questions

Page 165 1. Jules brings her gifts from everyone in the neighborhood. He also brings a tape of all the neighborhood sounds. SUMMARY
2. He asks them to help. They all like Mrs. Lee, so they are happy to help. INTERPRETATION
3. Accept reasonable responses. TASK

Sounds All Around

These events are from "Sounds All Around." They are out of order. Put a number in front of each one to show the right order.

_____ Mr. Jones draws on the sidewalk.

_____ Jules thinks of a plan.

_____ Jules plays a tape for Mrs. Lee.

_____ The rain makes a mess of the chalk drawings.

Now write each event next to an X in the order it happened. Fill in the other lines by telling what else happened in the story.

_____

_____

X _____

X _____

X _____

_____

_____

X _____

_____

Harcourt

The Little Lighthouse

by Kaye Gager   Use with *Blue Skies*, pages 166–173.

Preteaching Skills: Long Vowel /ō/ow, oa

Teach/Model

IDENTIFY THE SOUND Have children repeat the following sentence three times: *Tom and Joan row the boat to tow the float home.* Have them tell which words in the sentence have the /ō/ sound. (*Joan, row, boat, tow, float, home*)

ASSOCIATE LETTERS TO THEIR SOUNDS On the board, write the sentence *Tom and Joan row the boat to tow the float home.* Circle the word *Tom* and point out the CVC pattern. Remind children that in the word *Tom*, the *o* stands for the short *o* sound. Then circle the word *home*, and point out the CVC*e* pattern. Remind children that in the word *home*, the *o-e* stands for the long *o* sound. Circle *Joan, boat,* and *float,* and ask how these three words are alike. (*same vowel sound; /ō/ sound; letters* oa) Then ask how *Joan, boat,* and *float* are like *home.* (*long* o *sound*) Then tell children that the letters *oa* often stand for the /ō/ sound they hear in *Joan, boat,* and *float.* Then follow a similar procedure with the letters *ow* in *row* and *tow.*

WORD BLENDING Write *goat* on the board. Model blending sounds to read *goat.* Slide your hand under the word as you slowly elongate the sounds. Then read the word naturally. Have children blend sounds to read aloud these words: *soap, bowl, grow.*

Practice/Apply

APPLY THE SKILL *Vowel and Consonant Substitution* Write the first word in each pair below on the board, and have children read it aloud. Make the changes necessary to form the word in parentheses. Have children read each new word.

may (mow)	cot (coat)	she (show)	gray (grow)
tea (tow)	got (goat)	rod (road)	flat (float)

DICTATION AND WRITING Have children number a sheet of paper 1–8. Write *load* on the board. Tell children that in the words you say, /ō/ is spelled *oa* as in *load.* Dictate the words and have children write them. After they have finished, write each word on the board so children can proofread their work. Have them draw a line through a misspelled word and write the correct spelling above it.

1. float*	2. soaked*	3. throat	4. soap	*Word appears in
5. boat*	6. coat	7. coach	8. toast	"The Little Lighthouse."

Tell children that in the following sentence, /ō/ is spelled *ow.* Dictate the sentence: *Show me the plants that grow in the snow.*

READ LONGER WORDS *Compound Words* Write the word *snowman* on the board. Remind children that they can often figure out longer words by looking for smaller words in them. Cover the word *man*, and have children read the word that is left. Follow a similar procedure with the word *man.* Model how to blend the two smaller words to read aloud the word *snowman.* Follow a similar procedure to have children read these words: *rowboat, snowball, railroad.*

REPRODUCIBLE STUDENT ACTIVITY PAGE

INDEPENDENT PRACTICE See the reproducible Student Activity on page 123.

The Little Lighthouse

Fill in the oval in front of the sentence that tells about the picture.

1 ⬭ Ron owns a white coat.
ㅤㅤ⬭ Ron rows a boat.
ㅤㅤ⬭ Ron is throwing a snowball.

2 ⬭ The plant is slow to grow.
ㅤㅤ⬭ Joan will eat some toast.
ㅤㅤ⬭ I see a flower in the snow.

3 ⬭ The bowl is round.
ㅤㅤ⬭ Tam shows Rick her new soap.
ㅤㅤ⬭ Rick knows Tam owns a ball.

4 ⬭ The coach is mowing the grass.
ㅤㅤ⬭ A girl throws the coat.
ㅤㅤ⬭ Joan has scored a goal.

5 ⬭ The log floats on a road.
ㅤㅤ⬭ Four toads sit in a row.
ㅤㅤ⬭ I see three toads and a goat.

6 ⬭ The truck can tow a boat.
ㅤㅤ⬭ A crow is on the truck.
ㅤㅤ⬭ Joan and Bob will tow a bowl.

Introducing Vocabulary

Apply word identification strategies.

IDENTIFY VOCABULARY WORDS Display the vocabulary words, and ask children to identify any they know. Remind children that they can sometimes figure out an unfamiliar word by thinking about spelling patterns, letter patterns, and word parts. Point out the CVC*e* pattern in *white*. Have children use this pattern to help them read the word aloud. Follow a similar procedure with the *ar* in *cart* and *park* and the CVC pattern in *bench*. Then point to and read each of the other words (*listen* and *quietly*) aloud. Have children read them aloud after you.

Check understanding.

Discuss the meanings of the vocabulary words. Then have children write the vocabulary words on a sheet of paper. Ask them to name the word that completes each sentence and to circle that word on their papers.

VOCABULARY DEFINED	

bench a long seat, often of wood or stone

cart a small, wheeled vehicle, like a wagon

listen to pay attention in order to hear something

park a piece of land with grass, trees, benches, and other things for people to enjoy

quietly silently; in a way that does not make much noise

white the lightest of all colors; the opposite of black

- **Tom goes for a walk in the ___.** (*park*)
- **Tom sees a woman pushing a small ___.** (*cart*)
- **The color of the cart is ___.** (*white*)
- **Tom sits on a wooden ___.** (*bench*)
- **He likes to ___ to the birds sing.** (*listen*)
- **Then he walks away ___.** (*quietly*)

Children may be unfamiliar with some of the words in the title of the selection that they will read. After distributing the vocabulary page, point to the title, "The Little Lighthouse," read it aloud, and have children read it with you.

NOTE: The following vocabulary words from "The Park Bench" are reinforced in "The Little Lighthouse." If children are unfamiliar with these words, point them out as you encounter them during reading: *still, mist* (p. 166); *drowsy, lively* (p. 168); *gentle* and *agreed* (p. 169).

REPRODUCIBLE STUDENT ACTIVITY PAGE

INDEPENDENT PRACTICE See the reproducible Student Activity on page 125.

Name _____

The Little Lighthouse

Read the story.

When there is thick, white fog, the lighthouse horn blows.

We listen for a storm. The wind is still.

I will put my cart in the boat.

I sat on this bench to look at boats.

I used to go to this park. I will miss it.

We quietly float to our new home.

Complete each sentence with an underlined word from above.

1. The horn blows when there is thick, _____ fog.

2. We _____ for the sounds of a storm.

3. The girl puts her _____ in the boat.

4. The girl used to sit on the _____.

5. She used to go to the _____.

6. The boat floats _____ to a new home.

Harcourt

Directed Reading

Page 166 Read aloud the title of the story. Invite children to share what they know about lighthouses. Then read aloud the first sentence on page 166. Have children read the rest of page 166 to find out why it is a sad day. **Why is it a sad day?** (*The family is moving away from the lighthouse.*) INFERENTIAL: CAUSE AND EFFECT **Why do you think the girl is sad to leave the lighthouse?** (Possible response: *It was her home.*) INFERENTIAL: SPECULATE

Page 167 Have children read page 167 to find out what the girl will miss. **What will the girl miss?** (*helping to look for boats that are lost in the fog*) LITERAL: NOTE DETAILS **Why is the lighthouse's light always on?** (*so boats can see*) LITERAL: NOTE DETAILS

Page 168 Have children read page 168 to find out about one of the mornings the girl remembers. **What kind of morning does the girl remember?** (Possible responses: *foggy; drowsy and still*) INFERENTIAL: DRAW CONCLUSIONS **What does it mean to say, *the morning was drowsy?*** (Possible response: *It means the weather was calm and quiet.*) CRITICAL: AUTHOR'S CRAFT/UNDERSTAND IMAGERY **How did the big boat get out of the fog?** (*It saw the light.*) INFERENTIAL: INTERPRET STORY EVENTS

Page 169 Have children read page 169 to find out what else the girl remembers from that morning. **What else does the girl remember?** (*A little boat was about to hit the rocks, so she yelled, and the lighthouse sounded its horn.*) INFERENTIAL: SUMMARIZE

Pages 170–171 Read aloud the first sentence of page 170. Then have children read the rest of pages 170 and 171 to find out how the lighthouse helped the girl. **How did the lighthouse help the girl?** (*She and her sister were at the park during a storm. They couldn't see and got lost. They heard the horn and followed the sound home.*) INFERENTIAL: SUMMARIZE

Page 172 Ask children to read page 172 to find out what will happen to the lighthouse. **What will happen to the lighthouse?** (*A new family will move in, watch for lost boats, and keep the light on.*) INFERENTIAL: SUMMARIZE **What does the girl hope?** (*that the new family will love the lighthouse*) LITERAL: NOTE DETAILS **What do you think the girl means when she says, "My sister and I will listen to it in our dreams"?** (Possible response: *They will dream about the lighthouse.*) INFERENTIAL: SPECULATE

SUMMARIZING THE SELECTION Help children summarize the story in three sentences. Encourage them to tell why the girl will miss the lighthouse in their summaries. (Accept reasonable responses: *The girl and her family are leaving the lighthouse, which was their home. The girl will miss watching for boats, seeing the light, and hearing the horn. She hopes a new family will love the lighthouse as much as she does.*) INFERENTIAL: SUMMARIZE

Answers to Think About It Questions

Page 173
1. The girl stands on the bench and shouts to the boats. The lighthouse shines its light and sounds its horn. SUMMARY
2. The girl is sad. She says she will miss her home and that she will think about it in her dreams. INTERPRETATION
3. Accept reasonable responses. TASK

Name _____

REPRODUCIBLE
STUDENT
ACTIVITY PAGE

The Little Lighthouse

Complete the puzzle using words from the box.

white	listen	cart	park	quietly	bench

Across

5. The girl puts a basket in her _____.

6. The girl and her family _____ for a storm.

Down

1. The girl and her family _____ float away from the lighthouse.

2. Boats can get lost in the thick, _____ fog.

3. The girl and her sister get lost at the _____.

4. The girl's _____ is next to the lighthouse.

Write the completed clues in story order on the lines below.

1. _____

2. _____

3. _____

4. _____

5. _____

6. _____

Harcourt

A Secret Place

by Linda Olivares   Use with *Blue Skies*, pages 174–181.

Preteaching Skills: Long Vowels /ē/e; /ī/i; /ō/o

Teach/Model

IDENTIFY THE SOUND Ask children to repeat the following sentence three times: *Can she help me find the old, gold blinds?* Ask children to name the words in the sentence that have a long vowel sound. (*she, me, find, old, gold, blinds*)

ASSOCIATE LETTERS TO THEIR SOUNDS On the board, write the sentence *Can she help me find the old, gold blinds?* Circle the words *she* and *me*, and ask how these two words are alike. (*same vowel sound, /ē/; letter e*) Tell children that in words like *she* and *me*, the *e* often stands for the long *e* sound. Have children repeat the words and listen for the /ē/ sound. Then follow a similar procedure with the letter *i* in *find* and *blinds* and the letter *o* in *old* and *gold*.

WORD BLENDING Write *fold* on the board. Model blending the sounds to read *fold*: Slide your hand under the word as you slowly elongate the sounds /ffōōlldd/. Then read the word *fold* naturally. Have children practice blending sounds to read aloud these words: *we, kind, mind, bold*.

Practice/Apply

APPLY THE SKILL *Vowel and Consonant Substitution* Write the first word in each pair below on the board, and have children read it aloud. Make the changes necessary to form the word in parentheses. Ask children then to read each new word.

mend (mind)	hay (he)	tail (told)	blend (blind)
say (so)	grand (grind)	may (me)	must (most)

DICTATION AND WRITING Have children number their papers 1–8. Dictate the following words, and have children write them. After children have finished, write the words on the board so children can proofread their work. Have them draw a line through a misspelled word and write the correct spelling below it.

1. she	2. no*	3. find*	4. old
5. we	6. kind	7. told	8. go

*Word appears in "A Secret Place."

Dictate the following sentence: *Mo told me that she will not mind the cold.*

READ LONGER WORDS *Open CVC* Write the word *moment* on the board. Remind children that they can often figure out longer words by looking for word parts within it. Cover the letters *ment*, and have children read the first part of the word. Follow a similar procedure to have them read the second part. Model how to blend the two parts to read aloud the longer word *moment*. Follow a similar procedure to have children blend word parts to read these longer words: *silent, pilot, program, spider.*

REPRODUCIBLE STUDENT ACTIVITY PAGE

INDEPENDENT PRACTICE See the reproducible Student Activity on page 129.

Name _____

A Secret Place

Read the story.

Coco sells watches and clocks. This morning, she sold a clock.

At lunch time, she sold a gold watch.

At six, it was time to go. Coco put on a coat. It was cold outside.

Coco closed the blinds. Then she went home.

Write the word that best completes each sentence.

1. _____ owns a store.

     Jo   Coco   Matt

2. First, she _____ a clock.

     song   sold   so

3. Then, she sold a _____ watch.

     got   told   gold

4. She put on a coat because it was _____.

     cold   clock   fold

5. At six, she closed the _____.

     bins   grinds   blinds

Harcourt

Introducing Vocabulary

Apply word identification strategies.

IDENTIFY VOCABULARY WORDS Display the vocabulary words, and ask children to identify the ones they know. Remind children that they can sometimes figure out an unfamiliar word by thinking about spelling patterns, letter patterns, and word parts. Point out the letters *ue* in *clues*. Have children use what they know about these letters to help them read the word. Then ask children to read the word aloud. Follow a similar procedure with the word *missing* by pointing out the CVC pattern. Then point out the letters *sm* and *all* in *small*. Point to and read each of the other vocabulary words aloud. (*chief, key, shiny*) Have children read them aloud after you.

Check understanding.

Discuss the meanings of the vocabulary words. Then ask children to write the vocabulary words on a sheet of paper. Have them name the word that answers each of the following questions and circle that word on their papers.

- **Who is the head of the fire department?** (*chief*)
- **What do you use to unlock a door?** (*key*)
- **What is the opposite of *dull*?** (*shiny*)
- **What word means "little"?** (*small*)
- **What word means "lost"?** (*missing*)
- **What do detectives look for?** (*clues*)

Children may be unfamiliar with some of the words in the title of the selection that they will read. After distributing the vocabulary page, point to the title, "A Secret Place," read it aloud, and have children read it with you.

REPRODUCIBLE STUDENT ACTIVITY PAGE

INDEPENDENT PRACTICE See the reproducible Student Activity on page 131.

NOTE: The following vocabulary words from "The Pine Park Mystery" are reinforced in "A Secret Place." If children are unfamiliar with these words, point them out as you encounter them during reading: *typical, caused* (p. 174); *objects* (p. 176); *confused, clasp* (p. 177); *remove* (p. 179); and *cornered* (p. 180).

A Secret Place

Write a word from the box to complete each sentence.

small	missing	chief	key	shiny	clues

1. Jo said, "My blocks are _____! I can't find them anywhere!"

2. Lee said, "Where is my toy car? I just washed it so it's nice and _____."

3. Mom said, "I can't find the _____ to my car. Where did I put it?"

4. How are all the missing objects like each other? They are all _____ and can be hard to find.

5. How will Jo, Lee, and Mom find their things? They need to look for _____.

6. They will need a _____ to lead the hunt.

Harcourt

Directed Reading

Page 174 Read aloud the title of the play. Then have children read aloud the characters' names. Ask what a narrator is. Tell children to read page 174 to find out why it is not a typical day. **Why isn't it a typical day?** (*It is a snow day, so there is no school.*) INFERENTIAL: CAUSE-EFFECT **What happens while Jo and Lee are outside playing?** (*The blocks have been knocked over.*) INFERENTIAL: SEQUENCE

Page 175 Have children read page 175 to find out who Jo and Lee think took their things. **Who does Lee think took the car?** (*Jo*) **Who does Jo think took the blocks?** (*Lee*) INFERENTIAL: DRAW CONCLUSIONS **Where do the children think they put the things?** (*in their secret hiding places*) INFERENTIAL: DRAW CONCLUSIONS **Who do the children call?** (*Mom*) **Why?** (Accept reasonable responses.) CRITICAL: SPECULATE

Page 176 Have children read page 176 to find out what Mom tells the children. **What does Mom tell the children?** (Possible response: *She tells them to look for clues to find the missing things.*) INFERENTIAL: SUMMARIZE **What do the children think of Mom's idea?** (Possible response: *They think it's a good idea.*) INFERENTIAL: DRAW CONCLUSIONS **Who is Wags?** (*a dog*) INFERENTIAL: DRAW CONCLUSIONS/NOTE PICTURE CLUES

Page 177 Have children read page 177 to find out why Mom comes back. **Why does Mom come back?** (*She is confused; she is missing her car key.*) INFERENTIAL: DRAW CONCLUSIONS **Where do you think all the missing objects are?** (Accept reasonable responses.) INFERENTIAL: MAKE PREDICTIONS

Pages 178–179 Have children read pages 178–179 to find out whether the children find the toys. **Do Lee and Jo find the missing objects?** (*no*) **What do they do?** (*They start to clean up.*) INFERENTIAL: INTERPRET STORY EVENTS **What do you think the lumps in Wags's bed might be?** (*the missing objects*) INFERENTIAL: MAKE PREDICTIONS

Page 180 Have children read page 180 to confirm their predictions about Wags's bed. **What are the lumps in Wags's bed?** (*the missing objects*) INFERENTIAL: CONFIRM PREDICTIONS **Why does Jo say, "Now we know Wags has a secret hiding place of his own"?** (Accept reasonable responses.) INFERENTIAL: SUMMARIZE

SUMMARIZING THE SELECTION Ask students to think about what happened at the beginning, the middle, and the end of "A Secret Place." Then help them to summarize the story in three or four sentences. (Possible response: *Lee and Jo are missing some toys. Each thinks the other took the toys. They look for the toys but cannot find them. Then they pick up Wags's blanket, and the toys fall out.*) INFERENTIAL: SUMMARIZE

Answers to Think About It Questions

Page 181 1. They don't know that the missing things are hidden in Wags's bed. SUMMARY
2. They are surprised and happy to find the missing things. They say that they don't mind and that they will know where to look next time. INTERPRETATION
3. Accept reasonable responses. TASK

Name _____

A Secret Place

Complete the chart with words from the box to tell what happened in "A Secret Place."

small	missing	chief	key	shiny	clues

A toy car and some blocks were _____missing____. →

A ____key____ was lost, too. →

Mom said, "You need to look for ____clues____."

Jo was the ____chief____ and Lee was the helper. →

Lee said a ____shiny____ gold key would be easy to spot. →

Wags was a ____small____ dog, but he was very smart.

Answer these questions to tell about the rest of the story.

1. What were the missing things? ____toy car, blocks, key____

_____

2. Who had the missing things? ____Wags the dog____

3. Who found the missing things? ____Jo and Lee____

4. Think of another way the family could have found the missing things. Write it here. ____Responses may vary.____

_____

Harcourt

Hello from Here

by Deborah Eaton   **Use with *Blue Skies*, pages 182–189.**

Preteaching Skills: Long Vowel /ī/y

Teach/Model

IDENTIFY THE SOUND Ask children to repeat the following sentence three times: *Ty will try to fly five kites in the sky.* Have them identify the words that have the /ī/ sound. (*Ty, try, fly, five, kites, sky*)

ASSOCIATE LETTERS TO THEIR SOUNDS On the board, write the sentence *Ty will try to fly five kites in the sky.* Circle the words *five* and *kites*, and ask how they are alike. (*long* i *sound; same vowel sound*) Remind children that the letters *i-e* (CVC*e*) usually stand for the long *i* sound. Then circle the words *Ty, fly,* and *sky*, and ask how these words are alike. (*Same vowel sound; all end in* y.) Ask how these words are like *five* and *kites.* (*long* i *sound*) Underline the letter *y* in *Ty, fly,* and *sky.* Tell children that the letter *y* can sometimes act as a vowel and that when it does, it can stand for the /ī/ sound they hear in *Ty, fly,* and *sky.* Have children repeat the words and listen for the /ī/ sound.

WORD BLENDING Write *spy* on the board. Model blending the sounds to read *spy.* Slide your hand under the word as you slowly elongate the sounds. Then read the word naturally. Have children practice blending sounds to read aloud these words: *why, by, shy.*

Practice/Apply

APPLY THE SKILL *Vowel Substitution* Write the first word in each pair below on the board, and have children read it aloud. Make the changes necessary to form the words in parentheses. Have children read each new word.

free (fry)	tree (try)	be (by)	stay (sty)
she (shy)	flow (fly)	crow (cry)	me (my)

DICTATION AND WRITING Tell children to number their papers 1–8. Dictate the words, and have children write them. After they have finished, write each word on the board so children can proofread their work. Have them draw a line through a misspelled word and write the correct spelling below it.

1. fly	2. sky*	3. try	4. why*	*Word appears in
5. dry	6. cry	7. by*	8. my*	"Hello from Here."

Dictate the following sentence: *Why do birds fly by in the sky?*

READ LONGER WORDS *Change y to i Before Endings* Write on the board the sentence *I try to ride* and have children read it with you. Then write this sentence below it: *Jack tries to ride.* Read it aloud to children. Remind them that they can figure out a new word like *tries* by first looking for word parts they know within it. Point out the ending *-es.* Then model changing the *y* in *try* to *i* before adding *es.* Explain that in many words that end in *y,* you change the *y* to *i* before adding the ending *-es* or *-ed.* Write the word *try,* and have children read it aloud. Then write the word *tries* on the board. Cover the *tri* in *tries* to have children read aloud the ending *-es.* Finally, blend the two word parts to read aloud the word *tries.* Follow a similar procedure with these words: *fried, skies, dragonflies.*

REPRODUCIBLE STUDENT ACTIVITY PAGE

INDEPENDENT PRACTICE See the reproducible Student Activity on page 135.

Hello from Here

Write the word that best completes each sentence.

by	fly	dry	Why	tries	sky	cries	shy

1. Little Robin sees birds up in the _____.

2. He wants to _____ in the sky, too.

3. _____ is flying so hard?

4. Little Robin feels a little bit _____.

5. Now he is wet, but he wants to be _____.

6. Little Robin _____ hard.

7. He _____ to fly again.

8. Now Little Robin can fly all _____ himself!

Harcourt

Introducing Vocabulary

Apply word identification strategies.

IDENTIFY VOCABULARY WORDS Display the vocabulary words, and ask children to identify the ones they know. Remind children that they can sometimes figure out an unfamiliar word by looking for spelling patterns, letter patterns, smaller words, and word parts they know. Have children look for the smaller words they know in *grandchildren* and *mailbox*. If necessary, point out the CVC patterns in *grandchildren* and the CVVC and CVC patterns in *mailbox*. Have children use what they know about these spelling patterns and about reading longer words to help them read *grandchildren* and *mailbox* aloud. Follow a similar procedure with the CVVC pattern in *street* and the CVC*e* pattern in the word *surprise*. Then point to and read the other vocabulary words aloud. (*party, years*) Have children read them aloud after you.

VOCABULARY DEFINED
grandchildren a person's children's children
mailbox a place where the letter carrier puts your mail
party a gathering of people who are getting together to celebrate or have fun
street a road
surprise something unexpected; to make someone astonished or surprised
years 12-month periods

Check understanding.

Have children write the vocabulary words on a sheet of paper. Have children name the word that answers each of the following questions and circle that word on their papers.

- **What will my children's children be to me?** (*grandchildren*)
- **How do many people celebrate a birthday?** (*party*)
- **What word completes this sentence:** *Is Frances eight ___old?* (*years*)
- **What do you say when someone comes to a party they didn't know about?** (*surprise*)
- **Where does the letter carrier put some people's mail?** (*mailbox*)
- **What is another name for a road?** (*street*)

Children may be unfamiliar with some of the words in the title of the selection that they will read. After distributing the vocabulary page, point to the title, "Hello from Here," read it aloud, and have children read it with you.

REPRODUCIBLE STUDENT ACTIVITY PAGE

INDEPENDENT PRACTICE See the reproducible Student Activity on page 137.

NOTE: The following vocabulary words from "Good-bye, Curtis" are reinforced in "Hello from Here." If children are unfamiliar with these words, point them out as you encounter them during reading: *clerk* (p. 182); *pour* (p. 183); *addresses* (p. 184); *route, grown* (p. 185); and *honor* (p. 187).

Name ______________________________

REPRODUCIBLE STUDENT ACTIVITY PAGE

Hello from Here

Read the story. Then fill in the web. Use all the underlined words in your answers.

This street is like most streets. Lots of people live here—parents and children, grandparents and grandchildren. When there is a party, everyone is invited.

One day the kids get a big surprise. There is a postcard in every mailbox! Who sent them? There hasn't been this much fun in years!

Who lives there?

____

____

____

____

Where does the story take place?

____

Hello from Here

What are people invited to?

____

What is the big surprise?

____

____

____

____

Who sent the postcards? Read "Hello from Here" to find out.

Directed Reading

Page 182   Read aloud the title of the story. Ask children where they think someone is saying hello from. Then have children read page 182 to find out about Myles's street. **What is Myles's street like?** (*like most streets*) **Why?** (*The houses sit side by side; kids play in the yards.*) INFERENTIAL: MAKE COMPARISONS **Who lives on Myles's street?** (*Myles, Ms. Pryor, Mr. Clyde*) INFERENTIAL: DRAW CONCLUSIONS

Page 183   Read aloud the first sentence on page 183, and ask what children think the surprise might be. Have them read to find out. **What is the surprise?** (*The children on the boy's street started getting a lot of mail.*) INFERENTIAL: DRAW CONCLUSIONS **Who is the postcard from?** (*It does not say.*) INFERENTIAL: UNDERSTAND AUTHOR'S PURPOSE **What is the person writing the postcard doing?** (*sky diving*) INFERENTIAL: DRAW CONCLUSIONS

Page 184   Have children read page 184 to find out where the second postcard is from. **Where is this postcard from?** (*the desert*) INFERENTIAL: DRAW CONCLUSIONS **How would you answer the two questions on page 184?** (Accept reasonable responses.) INFERENTIAL: SPECULATE

Page 185   Have children read page 185 to find out what Myles does to find answers to his questions. **What does Myles do?** (*He tries to think like a spy and look for clues.*) LITERAL: NOTE DETAILS **What clues does Myles find?** (*The postcards have no stamps.*) **How does the clue help Myles?** (*He knows that they are not coming through the mail.*) INFERENTIAL: SYNTHESIZE **Who do you think Myles catches?** (Accept reasonable responses.) INFERENTIAL: MAKE PREDICTIONS

Page 186   Have children read page 186 to find out whom Myles catches at the mailbox. **Who does Myles catch?** (*Mr. Clyde*) LITERAL: NOTE DETAILS **Why is Mr. Clyde sending the cards?** (*He is doing it for fun.*) INFERENTIAL: CAUSE AND EFFECT

Page 187   Ask children to read page 187 to find out about this postcard. **Who writes this postcard?** (*Myles*) LITERAL: NOTE DETAILS **Why does Myles send this postcard?** (*to invite the children to Mr. Clyde's birthday party*) LITERAL: NOTE DETAILS **Why do you think Myles is having a party for Mr. Clyde?** (Possible response: *Myles wants to do something nice for Mr. Clyde.*) INFERENTIAL: INTERPRET CHARACTERS' MOTIVATIONS

SUMMARIZING THE SELECTION Ask children to think about Myles's mystery, his clues, and his solution. Then help them summarize the story in a few sentences.

Answers to Think About It Questions

Page 188   1. Mr. Clyde likes the children. He feels as if they are his grandchildren. He sends them postcards. SUMMARY
2. Myles likes Mr. Clyde but feels a little sorry for him because Mr. Clyde is lonely. Myles decides to have a birthday party for Mr. Clyde. INTERPRETATION
3. Accept reasonable responses. TASK

Page 189   For instruction on the Focus Skill: Summarize, see page 189 in *Blue Skies*.

Name _____

Hello from Here

Write a word to complete the sentences about the story.

1. Mr. Clyde had no _____.

              mailbox   car   grandchildren

2. Mr. Clyde gave the kids a big _____.

                     surprise   cake   party

3. One boy hid by a _____ to find out who sent
the postcards.   **car   mailbox   house**

4. He saw Mr. Clyde coming up the _____.

                     street   steps   ramp

5. Mr. Clyde had waited _____ to try sky diving.

               what   days   years

6. The kids had a _____ for Mr. Clyde.

         card   kite   party

Write answers to these questions.

7. What clues did the boy use to find out who was sending

    the postcards? _____

8. Why did the boy send cards to the kids on his street?

_____

9. What would you do to thank Mr. Clyde for the postcards?

_____

Harcourt

Selection Comprehension • Grade 2 **139**

Phonics

The Music Maker

by Sydnie Meltzer Kleinhenz   Use with *Blue Skies*, pages 190–197.

Preteaching Skills: Long Vowel /ī/*igh*

Teach/Model

IDENTIFY THE SOUND Have children repeat the following sentence three times: *Mike likes to see bright lights high in the sky at night.* Ask children to identify the words that have the /ī/ sound. (*Mike, likes, bright, lights, high, sky, night*)

ASSOCIATE LETTERS TO THEIR SOUNDS On the board, write the sentence *Mike likes to see bright lights high in the sky at night.* Circle the words *Mike, likes,* and *sky,* and ask how they are alike. (*long i sound; same vowel sound*) Remind children that the letters *i-e* (CVC*e*) and *y* often stand for the long *i* sound. Then circle the words *bright, lights, high,* and *night,* and ask how these four words are alike. (*Same vowel sound; all have igh in them.*) Tell children that when *i* is followed by the letters *gh,* the *igh* usually stands for the /ī/ sound they hear in *bright, lights, high,* and *night.* Have children repeat the words and listen for the /ī/ sound.

WORD BLENDING Write *might* on the board. Model blending the sounds to read *might:* Slide your hand under the word as you slowly elongate the sounds /mmīītt/. Then read the word *might* naturally. Have children practice blending sounds to read aloud these words: *fright, sigh, tight.*

Practice/Apply

APPLY THE SKILL *Vowel Substitution* Write the first word in each pair below on the board, and have children read the words aloud. Make the changes necessary to form the word in parentheses. Then have children read each new word.

mat (might)	rat (right)	flat (flight)	lit (light)
say (sigh)	sit (sight)	he (high)	neat (night)

DICTATION AND WRITING Have children number a sheet of paper 1–8. Dictate the following words, and have children write them. After children write each word, write it on the board so they can proofread their work. Have them draw a line through a misspelled word and write the correct spelling below it.

1. night   2. right*   3. bright   4. high*
5. tight*   6. light   7. flight   8. spotlight*

*Word appears in "The Music Maker."

Dictate the following sentence: *The bright light gave me a fright last night.*

READ LONGER WORDS *Compound Words* Write the word *nighttime* on the board. Tell children that they can often figure out longer words by looking for smaller words in them. Cover the word *time,* and have children read aloud the word *night.* Follow a similar procedure to have children read the word *time.* Then blend the two smaller words to read aloud the word *nighttime.* Follow the same procedure with the words *flashlight, highway,* and *tightrope.*

REPRODUCIBLE STUDENT ACTIVITY PAGE

INDEPENDENT PRACTICE See the reproducible Student Activity on page 141.

The Music Maker

Write the word that makes the sentence tell about the picture.

1. "Let's take a walk to the _____lighthouse_____,"
   said Mom.

   nightshirt   nighttime   lighthouse

2. "How will we find the path at _____night_____?"
   asked Tim.

   fight   night   tight

3. "We will use a _____flashlight_____," Mom
   replied.

   flashlight   lightning   highway

4. The lighthouse sits _____high_____ up on a cliff.

   sight   hide   high

5. It has a big _____light_____ at the top.

   flight   light   like

6. The light is very _____bright_____.

   bride   might   bright

7. The light shows ships the _____right_____ way
   to go.

   ride   right   rind

8. Ann tells her mom, "I _____might_____ work
   there someday."

   might   night   light

Introducing Vocabulary

Apply word identification strategies.

IDENTIFY VOCABULARY WORDS Display the vocabulary words, and ask children to identify the ones they know. Remind children that they can sometimes figure out an unfamiliar word by thinking about spelling patterns, letter patterns, and word parts. Have children look for the CVC pattern in the words *boxes*, *bucket*, and *sticks*. Then have children use what they know about the CVC pattern to help them read the words *boxes*, *bucket*, and *sticks* aloud. Follow a similar procedure with the vowels *ou* in *clouds*. Then point to and read the other vocabulary words aloud. (*answered*, *garbage can*) Have children read them aloud after you.

Check understanding.

Discuss the meanings of the vocabulary words. Then ask children to write the vocabulary words on a sheet of paper. Have them name the word that answers each of the following questions and circle that word on their papers.

- **What word completes this sentence:** *Have you ___ my question?* (*answered*)
- **What do people use to play the drums?** (*sticks*)
- **What might you use to carry water?** (*bucket*)
- **What are made of tiny drops of water?** (*clouds*)
- **What might you put your trash in?** (*garbage can*)
- **What might you pack things in when you move to a new home?** (*boxes*)

Children may be unfamiliar with some of the words in the title of the selection that they will read. After distributing the vocabulary page, point to the title, "The Music Maker," read it aloud, and have children read it with you.

REPRODUCIBLE STUDENT ACTIVITY PAGE

INDEPENDENT PRACTICE See the reproducible Student Activity on page 143.

NOTE: The following vocabulary words from "Max Found Two Sticks" are reinforced in "The Music Maker." If children are unfamiliar with these words, point them out as you encounter them during reading: *rhythm* (p. 190); *startled*, *appeared* (p. 192); *imitated* (p. 194); *created* (p. 195); and *conductor* (p. 196).

Name _____

The Music Maker

Read the ad.

This is Dwight. He plays the drums. Dwight takes his **sticks** everywhere. He can drum on **boxes**. He can drum on a **bucket**.

He can even drum on a **garbage can**! Dwight would drum on **clouds** if he could.

Dwight says he can make music with his drumsticks. His friends asked him how. Dwight **answered** that he needed the right kind of drum.

What kind of drum can that be? Find out as you read "The Music Maker."

Write one or more words from the ad to complete each sentence. Choose from the words in dark type.

1. Dwight likes to drum on _____ boxes _____, a

   _____ bucket _____, and a _____ garbage can _____.

2. Dwight uses _____ sticks _____ to bang out sounds.

3. Dwight can't drum on _____ clouds _____.

4. After Dwight's friends asked him something, Dwight

   _____ answered _____ them.

Harcourt

Directed Reading

Page 190   Read aloud the story title. Ask children who they think the music maker is and what music he might make. Then have them read page 190 to find out. **Who is the music maker?** (*Dwight*) INFERENTIAL: DRAW CONCLUSIONS   **What does he make music on?** (Possible responses: *anything he could find; boxes*) INFERENTIAL: USE CONTEXT AND PICTURE CLUES

Page 191   Have children read page 191 to find out what Dwight is doing. **What is Dwight doing?** (*He is tapping on a bucket and is trying to get the right sound with his drumsticks.*) INFERENTIAL: UNDERSTAND CHARACTERS' ACTIONS   **What do you think Dwight will try his drumsticks on next?** (Accept reasonable responses.) INFERENTIAL: MAKE PREDICTIONS

Page 192   Have children read the page to find out what Dwight tries next. **What does Dwight try his drumsticks on next?** (*a garbage can lid*) LITERAL: NOTE DETAILS **Why are the children covering their ears?** (Possible response: *The noise from the garbage can lid drum is too loud.*) INFERENTIAL: CAUSE AND EFFECT

Page 193   Have children read page 193 to find out why Dwight is working on his music. **Why is Dwight working on his music?** (*He is going to play "The Star-Spangled Banner" at the baseball game.*) INFERENTIAL: UNDERSTAND CHARACTERS' MOTIVATION   **Does Linda think he will be able to play the notes on a drum?** (*no*) **Do you?** (Accept reasonable responses.) SPECULATE

Page 194   Have children read page 194 to find out what instruments Jon thinks Dwight would need to play real music. **What instruments does Jon think Dwight needs to play real music?** (*a trumpet or a flute*) LITERAL: NOTE DETAILS   **What do you think Dwight will show Jon and Linda?** (Accept reasonable responses.) INFERENTIAL: MAKE PREDICTIONS

Page 195   Have children read page 195 to find out what Dwight shows his friends. **What does Dwight show his friends?** (Possible response: *He shows them how to make a steel drum.*) INFERENTIAL: INTERPRET STORY EVENTS   **What steps does Dwight's dad follow?** (*He heats a tin can, hammers shapes into the top, and then puts the can in water.*) INFERENTIAL: NOTE SEQUENCE   **What happens when Dwight taps on the drum?** (*Notes sound.*) LITERAL: NOTE DETAILS

Page 196   Have children read page 196 to find out what happens before the baseball game. **What happens before the baseball game?** (*The band plays "The Star-Spangled Banner." Dwight makes music on his drum.*) INFERENTIAL: SEQUENCE   **How do you think Dwight feels after he plays on his steel drum for the fans?** (Possible responses: *He feels proud because he has played well and entertained the crowd; he feels happy because he likes playing music.*) CRITICAL: IDENTIFY WITH CHARACTERS

SUMMARIZING THE SELECTION Ask children to think about what happens first, next, and last in the story. Then help them summarize the story in a few sentences.

Answers to Think About It Questions

Page 197   1. Dwight can play a tune on his drum. He can play "real music." SUMMARY
2. Dwight feels proud of his dad's drums. He shows them to his friends, and he plays one at the baseball game. INTERPRETATION
3. Accept reasonable responses. TASK

Name _____

REPRODUCIBLE
STUDENT
ACTIVITY PAGE

The Music Maker

Write a word on each line. Complete the story strip to show the order of events in "The Music Maker."

Dwight put rubber bands on his _____. **sticks drum**	First, Dwight drummed on his _____. **bucket boxes**	Next, Dwight drummed on the _____. **bucket basket**
When Dwight drummed on a _____, **garbage can box** he gave his friends a fright.	Dwight planned to play a tune at the _____ **game show** on Saturday.	Linda said, "You can't play a _____ **rhythm tune** with a drum."
Dwight _____, **answered danced** "Yes, I can."	Dwight's dad _____ **made bought** steel drums.	When he put the heated can in water, _____ **drops clouds** of steam came up.

Harcourt

Selection Comprehension • Grade 2   **145**

Rodeo!

by Robert Newell   **Use with *Blue Skies*, pages 198–205.**

Preteaching Skills: Long Vowel /ē/y, *ie*

Teach/Model

IDENTIFY THE SOUND Have children repeat the following sentence aloud three times: *The happy chief sees thirty puppies.* Ask children to identify the words that have the /ē/ sound. (*happy, chief, sees, thirty, puppies*)

ASSOCIATE LETTERS TO THEIR SOUNDS On the board, write the sentence *The happy chief sees thirty puppies.* Circle the word *sees*, and ask children to read it aloud. Remind them that the letters *ee* usually stand for the /ē/ sound. Then circle the words *happy* and *thirty*, and ask how these two words are alike. (*same vowel sound at the end; both end in* y; *long* e *sound*) Remind children that *y* can stand for the long *e* sound. Then follow a similar procedure with the letters *ie* and the words *chief* and *puppies.*

WORD BLENDING Write *bunnies* on the board. Model blending the sounds to read *bunnies.* Slide your hand under the word as you slowly elongate the sounds. Then read the word naturally. Have children practice blending sounds to read aloud these words: *thief, pennies, fluffy.*

Practice/Apply

APPLY THE SKILL *Vowel Substitution* Write the first word in each pair of words below on the board, and have children read it aloud. Make the changes necessary to form the word in parentheses. Have children read each new word.

parts (parties)   tide (tidy)   shine (shiny)
happen (happy)   stores (stories)   tin (tiny)

DICTATION AND WRITING Have children number their papers 1–8. Write *study* on the board and tell children that in the words you say, the long *e* sound is spelled *y* as in *study.* Dictate the words and have children write them. After they write each word, write it on the board so children can proofread their work. Have them draw a line through a misspelled word and write the correct spelling below it.

1. risky*   2. pony*   3. muddy*   4. thirsty   *Word appears
5. handy*   6. tricky*   7. party   8. candy   in "Rodeo!"

Tell children that in the following sentence, /ē/ will be spelled *ie.* Dictate the sentence: *The thief met briefly with the chief.*

READ LONGER WORDS *Double Consonants* Write the word *sunny* on the board. Tell children that they can often figure out longer words by looking for word parts they know. Ask children what smaller word they see in this word. (*sun*) Then blend the word *sun* with the word part *ny* to read aloud the word *sunny.* Remind children that a longer word with double consonants, such as *sunny*, can be divided into syllables between those consonants. Children can decode each syllable and then blend them together to read the longer word. Follow this procedure to have children blend word parts to read these longer words: *pennies, bubbly, frilly.*

REPRODUCIBLE STUDENT ACTIVITY PAGE

INDEPENDENT PRACTICE See the reproducible Student Activity on page 147.

Rodeo!

Complete each sentence with a word from the box.

chilly	sleepy	puppies	dirty
Fluffy	family	hungry	happy

1. Penny asks, "Mom, may I have one of the _____?"

2. Mom asks, "Penny, will you feed the puppy when he is _____?"

3. "Will you wash the puppy when he is _____?"

4. "Will you walk the puppy when it is _____ outside?"

5. "Will you play with the puppy at night when you are _____?"

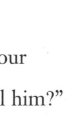

6. Penny says, "Yes, Mom. The puppy will be very _____ with me."

7. Mom says, "Now the puppy is a part of our _____. What will you call him?"

8. Penny says, "I will call him _____!"

Harcourt

Introducing Vocabulary

Apply word identification strategies.

IDENTIFY VOCABULARY WORDS Display the vocabulary words, and ask children to identify the ones they know. Remind children that they can sometimes figure out an unfamiliar word by looking for spelling patterns, letter patterns, and word parts. Have children use what they know about CVC*e* to help them read *ride* and *rope* aloud. Follow a similar procedure with the letters *or* in *horse* and the smaller words in *birthday*. (*birth/day*) Remind children that the letter *y* can sometimes act as a vowel and that when it does, it can stand for the /ī/ sound. Then have them read *style* aloud. Finally, point to and read the word *practice* aloud. Have children read it aloud after you.

VOCABULARY DEFINED
birthday the day that marks someone's or something's birth or beginning
horse a large animal that you can ride that has four legs, four hoofs, a mane, and a tail
practice to do something over and over to get better at it
ride to stay on a horse or another animal while it moves
rope a long, braided cord
style a special way in which something is done

Check understanding.

Discuss the meanings of the vocabulary words with children. Then have children write each vocabulary word on a sheet of paper. Ask children to name the word that answers each of the following questions and to circle that word on their papers.

- **What is July 4th for the United States?** (*birthday*)
- **What should you do if you want to get better at something?** (*practice*)
- **What animal has a mane?** (*horse*)
- **What can you use for tying knots?** (*rope*)
- **What do you do on a horse?** (*ride*)
- **Which word completes this sentence: *What is your dancing ___ ?*** (*style*)

Children may be unfamiliar with the word *Rodeo*, which is the title of the selection that they will read. After distributing the vocabulary page, point to the title, read it aloud, and have children read it with you. Then discuss its meaning.

REPRODUCIBLE STUDENT ACTIVITY PAGE

INDEPENDENT PRACTICE See the reproducible Student Activity on page 149.

NOTE: The following vocabulary words from "Anthony Reynoso: Born to Rope" are reinforced in "Rodeo!" If students are unfamiliar with these words, point them out as you encounter them during reading: *dappled, exhibition* (p. 198); *ranch, landscape* (p. 199); *thousands* (p. 200); and *business* (p. 201).

Name _____

Rodeo!

Read the ad.

Come to the Rodeo!

Watch cowboys <u>ride</u> bucking broncos.

Watch a cowgirl ride a <u>horse</u>
   as she throws her <u>rope</u>!

Watch riders <u>practice</u> their skills
   with <u>style</u>!

Do you know someone who
   has a <u>birthday</u> coming up?

A trip to the rodeo is the best birthday surprise!

Write a word from the ad to complete each sentence. Choose from the underlined words.

1. Rodeo cowboys must hold on tight when they

_____ a bucking bronco.

2. Cowboys must _____ their riding skills.

3. It takes a lot of practice to ride with _____.

4. That cowgirl is on a very tall _____.

5. The cowgirl swings her _____

and throws it as she rides.

6. A trip to the rodeo is a good surprise for someone's

_____.

Harcourt

Directed Reading

Page 198 Read aloud the story title. Ask what a rodeo is, and explain that children will learn more about rodeos as they read. Then have children read page 198 to find out about a rodeo. **What do you think people in a rodeo wear, use, and ride?** (Possible response: *They wear ten-gallon hats, they use ropes, and they ride dappled ponies.*) INFERENTIAL: DRAW CONCLUSIONS **What does *dappled* mean?** (*spotted*) INFERENTIAL: USE PICTURE CLUES

Page 199 Have children read page 199 to find out some things cowboys do in rodeos. **What is one thing rodeo cowboys do?** (*try to ride a bucking horse for eight seconds*) INFERENTIAL: DRAW CONCLUSIONS **Why can eight seconds be a "very long time"?** (Possible response: *When it is very difficult to do something, eight seconds seems like a long time.*) INFERENTIAL: UNDERSTAND FIGURATIVE LANGUAGE **Why can many rodeo riders practice every day?** (*They work on ranches.*) INFERENTIAL: CAUSE AND EFFECT **What does "Now he's seeing the landscape close up" mean?** (Possible response: *The cowboy is on the ground, so he is seeing the land up close.*) INFERENTIAL: UNDERSTAND FIGURATIVE LANGUAGE

Page 200 Have children read page 200 to find out about another rodeo event. **What is the rodeo event on this page called?** (*roping*) INFERENTIAL: INTERPRET STORY EVENTS **What is roping?** (*throwing a rope to catch an animal, like a cow*) INFERENTIAL: DRAW CONCLUSIONS **How does the pony help?** (*It backs up to keep the rope tight.*) LITERAL: NOTE DETAILS

Page 201 Have children read page 201 to find out what event this person is doing. **What event did you read about on this page?** (*riding a bull*) INFERENTIAL: MAIN IDEA

Page 202 Ask children why a clown might be at a rodeo. Have them read page 202 to find out. **What do clowns do at a rodeo?** (*They keep cowboys and cowgirls safe; they keep horses and bulls away from riders who have fallen.*) INFERENTIAL: SUMMARIZE

Page 203 Have children read page 203 to find out about the rodeo's birthday. **When is the rodeo's birthday?** (*July 4*) **What else has a birthday on July 4?** (*the United States*) LITERAL: NOTE DETAILS **How might someone wish the rodeo a happy birthday?** (Responses will vary.) INFERENTIAL: SPECULATE

SUMMARIZING THE SELECTION Ask children to think about what they learned about rodeos. Then help them summarize the selection. (Possible response: *There are many events in a rodeo. People ride bucking horses; people rope animals; and people ride bulls. People dressed as clowns help keep the riders safe. The rodeo is over 100 years old, and its birthday is on July 4.*) INFERENTIAL: SUMMARIZE

Answers to Think About It Questions

Page 204 1. Cowboys and cowgirls take part in bronco riding, roping, and bull riding. SUMMARY
2. The riders probably like the clowns and are glad the clowns are there because the clowns help keep the riders safe. INTERPRETATION
3. Accept reasonable responses. TASK

Page 205 For further instruction on the Focus Skill: Main Idea, see page 205 in *Blue Skies*.

Name _____

Rodeo!

Complete the puzzle with words from the box.

horse	practice	rope	ride	birthday	style

Across

1. Riding well takes a lot of ___.

4. A cowboy must ___ a bucking horse for 8 seconds.

5. A cowgirl's ___ helps her keep her rope tight.

6. ___ is not needed to ride a bull.

Down

2. A cowgirl may have thrown her ___ thousands of times.

3. July 4 is the rodeo's ___.

Write the completed clues on the lines below.

Riding well takes a lot of practice

A cowboy must ride a bucking horse for 8 seconds.

A cowgirl's horse helps her keep her rope tight.

Style is not needed to ride a bull.

A cowgirl may have thrown her rope thousands of times.

July 4 is the rodeo's birthday.

_____

_____

Harcourt

Phonics

Zelda Moves to the Desert

by Linda Lott   Use with *Blue Skies*, pages 206–213.

Preteaching Skills: Consonant /j/ge, gi, gy, dge

Teach/Model

IDENTIFY THE SOUND Read aloud the following sentence: *Gemma ate fudge in the giant gym.* Ask children to identify the words in the sentence that have the /j/ sound. (*Gemma, fudge, giant, gym*) Then have them raise their hands each time they hear a word with the /j/ sound: *gum, gem, gave, gym, giant, got.*

ASSOCIATE LETTERS TO THEIR SOUNDS Write the sentence *Gemma ate fudge in the giant gym* on the board and have a volunteer underline the words that contain the letter *g*. Tell children that the letter *g* usually stands for the /j/ sound when it is followed by *e, i,* or *y*. Point to the word *fudge* and tell children that the letters *dge* usually stand for the /j/ sound.

WORD BLENDING Model reading the word *gym* by blending the sounds the letters stand for: Slide your hand under the letters as you slowly blend the sounds /ggyymm/. Then read the word *gym* naturally and have children do the same. Help children form a generalization about the /g/ and /j/ sounds spelled with *g*: When *g* is followed by an *e, i,* or *y*, it usually stands for the /j/ sound. When *g* is followed by *a, o,* or *u*, the *g* usually stands for the /g/ sound.

Practice/Apply

APPLY THE SKILL *Consonant and Vowel Substitution* Write on the board the first word in each pair below, one at a time, and have children read it. Then make the changes necessary to form each word in parentheses. Have volunteers take turns reading each new word aloud.

game (gym)   leg (ledge)   bug (budge)   gate (germ)
peg (page)   gas (gem)   hug (hedge)   gain (giant)

DICTATION AND WRITING Have children number their papers 1–8. Dictate the following words, and have children write them. After each word is written, write it on the board so children can proofread their work. They should draw a line through a misspelled word and write the correct spelling below it.

1. gym   2. gentle*   3. gems*   4. giant*   *Word appears in "Zelda
5. cage   6. age   7. edge*   8. ledge*   Moves to the Desert."

Dictate the following sentences: *Mary sees a gem by the hedge. The gem is red.*

READ LONGER WORDS *Open VCV* Write the words *gigantic* and *hotel* on the board. Remind children that when they come across a word that has the VCV pattern, they should try saying the first syllable with a short vowel sound and then a long vowel sound to see which one sounds right. Then model saying the first syllable in *gigantic* with first a short and then a long vowel sound. Then ask children which part of the word says /jī/, which part says /gan/, and which part says /tik/. Follow the same procedure with *hotel*. Then ask children to read the words *pilot* and *total* and explain how they figured them out.

REPRODUCIBLE STUDENT ACTIVITY PAGE

INDEPENDENT PRACTICE See the reproducible Student Activity on page 153.

Name _____

Zelda Moves to the Desert

Read this story. Circle the words that have the g sound you hear in *gem*.

Gerry and Ginny

Gerry thinks this is a good day to be outside. He walks past the hedge to the edge of the river. He sits under a giant tree. Gerry looks at the sky. He feels a gentle wind.

Ginny thinks this is a good day to be inside. She thinks it is going to rain. She wants to play inside. She goes to the gym to play games.

Use some of the words you circled to complete each sentence.

1. Gerry sits by the _____ of the river.

2. He is near a _____ tree.

3. There is a _____ wind.

4. _____ goes inside.

5. She wants to play games in the _____.

Introducing Vocabulary

Apply word identification strategies.

LOOK FOR FAMILIAR SPELLING PATTERNS Write the vocabulary words on the board, and ask volunteers to identify any they know. You may want to read aloud the words *flooded* and *mice* and have children repeat them after you. Remind children that they can figure out new words by looking for familiar spelling patterns and thinking about the sounds that the letters stand for.

Give children the following clues and have a volunteer say and frame the word that answers each one:

- **tells about a place that suddenly fills with water** (*flooded*)
- **a baby drinks milk from this** (*bottle*)
- **water that seems to roll along the shore** (*waves*)
- **more than one mouse** (*mice*)
- **tells what happened to something heavy that went under water** (*sank*)
- **wind blows into this part of a boat** (*sail*)

VOCABULARY DEFINED
bottle container for liquids, made of glass or plastic
flooded filled with water
mice more than one mouse
sail a piece of material, usually cloth, that catches the wind on a boat
sank went under water
waves curved swells of water

Check understanding.

Ask children to write the vocabulary words on a sheet of paper. Then ask the following questions. After children have named the correct word, they should circle that word on their papers.

> **Which word . . .**
> - **tells what water sometimes comes in?** (*bottle*)
> - **names the small, furry animals that cats like to chase?** (*mice*)
> - **tells what a rock did when it was thrown into a pond?** (*sank*)
> - **names the cloth that catches wind on a boat?** (*sail*)
> - **tells what happened to a street when it rained too much?** (*flooded*)
> - **names water that is moving in the ocean?** (*waves*)

Children may be unfamiliar with some of the words in the title of the selection they are about to read. After distributing the vocabulary page, point to the title, "Zelda Moves to the Desert," read it aloud, and have children read it with you.

NOTE: The following vocabulary words from "Montigue on the High Seas" are reinforced in "Zelda Moves to the Desert." If children are unfamiliar with these words, point them out as you encounter them during reading: *cozy, drifted* (p. 206); *realized* (p. 208); *looming, launched* (p. 209); *fleet* (p. 210); and *horizon* (p. 211).

REPRODUCIBLE STUDENT ACTIVITY PAGE

INDEPENDENT PRACTICE See the reproducible Student Activity on page 155.

Name _____

Zelda Moves to the Desert

Read each sentence. Write the word from the box that makes sense in the sentence.

mice	sail	waves	flooded	sank	bottle

Water came into Zelda's cave in

_____ .

Soon Zelda's cave was

_____ !

Zelda tossed a rock into the water, and it

_____ .

Zelda saw a

_____ float by.

Zelda saw

_____

in a boat with a

_____ .

What will Zelda do? Read the story to find out.

Harcourt

Directed Reading

Page 206

Help children read the title of the story aloud. Then have them describe what they see in the illustration. Point to the bat and tell children that this is Zelda, the main character. Ask children what kind of weather they see outside the cave. *(rain)* Then have children read page 206 to learn more about Zelda. **What does Zelda do at night?** (Possible response: *She goes out flying to find bugs to eat.*) LITERAL: NOTE DETAILS

Page 207

Have children look at the illustration on page 207 and read the text to find out what is happening to Zelda's home. Model the thinking: **It is raining harder, and Zelda's home will be flooded. Zelda looks scared. What do you think she will do next?** CRITICAL: MAKE PREDICTIONS

Pages 208–209

Have children read pages 208–209 to find out what Zelda does next. Read aloud the words *looming* and *launched* on page 209 and discuss their meanings. **What do the mice tell Zelda?** (Possible response: *They tell her to find a new home.*) LITERAL: NOTE DETAILS **What does Zelda decide to do?** (Possible response: *She decides to find a new home.*) INFERENTIAL: MAKE AND CONFIRM PREDICTIONS Model the thinking: **Zelda goes to the forest first, but she thinks it's too damp there. Where do you think she will go next?** (Responses will vary.) CRITICAL: MAKE PREDICTIONS

Page 210

Have children look at the illustration on page 210. Then have them read the page to confirm their predictions. If necessary, explain that a fleet of boats is a group of boats sailing or floating together. Then model the thinking: **Zelda flies out to the sea, but she thinks it's too wet to be a good home for her. I think she will look for a dry home next.**

Page 211

Point out the words *horizon* and *realized* in the first paragraph and help children break the words into syllables to read them. Explain that the horizon is the line where the sky and land or water seem to meet and that *realized* means "understood something." Then have a volunteer read aloud the first paragraph. Discuss with children what a desert is like. **Do you think Zelda will make the desert her new home? Why or why not?** (Possible response: *Yes, because the desert is dry and she is looking for a dry place to live.*) INFERENTIAL: MAKE PREDICTIONS Then ask children to read the rest of the page to confirm their predictions.

SUMMARIZING THE SELECTION Have children summarize the story by telling about Zelda's problem and how she solves it. (Possible response: *Zelda the bat lives in a cave with a creek. When it rains hard, her cave gets flooded. She decides to look for a new, dry home. She goes to the forest and to the sea, but these places are too damp or wet for her. She flies to the desert and makes a home there.*) INFERENTIAL: SUMMARIZE

Answers to Think About It Questions

Page 212

1. Zelda leaves her cave because it is not cozy or safe. She moves to the desert because it is safe, dry, and cozy. SUMMARY
2. Possible response: Zelda wouldn't like a home by a lake because she doesn't like the damp woods or the wet sea. INTERPRETATION
3. Accept reasonable responses. TASK

Page 213

For instruction on the Focus Skill: Cause and Effect, see page 213 in *Blue Skies*.

Name _____

Zelda Moves to the Desert

Complete the flowchart with words from the box to tell what happens in "Zelda Moves to the Desert."

waves	bottle	sank	flooded	sail	mice

Zelda left her home because it _____.

The heavy rain made _____ in the water.

A rock _____ far down in the water. Zelda knew it was deep.

Zelda saw a _____ float by.

Some _____ floated by in a bowl.

They lost the _____ for their boat.

Answer these questions to tell about the rest of the story.

1. Where did Zelda fly to first? _____

2. Was that a good home for her? Why not? _____
_____

3. Where did Zelda fly to next? _____

4. Was that a good home for her? Why not? _____
_____

5. Where did Zelda find her new home? _____

_____

Harcourt

When You Visit Relatives

by Hector Morales   Use with *Blue Skies*, pages 214–221.

Preteaching Skills: Vowel Diphthongs /oi/oi, oy

Teach/Model

IDENTIFY THE SOUND Have students repeat the following sentence three times: *Roy points to a coin in the soil by his toy.* Have children identify the words that have the /oi/ sound. (*Roy, points, coin, soil, toy*)

ASSOCIATE LETTERS TO THEIR SOUNDS On the board, write the sentence *Roy points to a coin in the soil by his toy.* Circle the words *Roy* and *toy*, and ask how these two words are alike. (*same vowel sound at the end; both end in* oy) Underline the letters *oy* in *Roy* and *toy*. Tell children that when the letters *oy* come together in a word, they usually stand for the /oi/ sound that children hear in *Roy* and *toy*. Then follow a similar procedure with the letters *oi* and the words *points, coin,* and *soil*.

WORD BLENDING Write *boil* on the board. Model blending the sounds to read *boil*. Slide your hand under the word as you slowly elongate the sounds /bboill/. Then read the word *boil* naturally. Have children practice blending sounds to read aloud the words *coil, joy, moist,* and *Troy*.

Practice/Apply

APPLY THE SKILL *Vowel Substitution* Write the first word in each of the following pairs on the board, and have children read each one aloud. Then make the changes necessary to form each word in parentheses. Ask children to read each new word.

sail (soil)	by (boy)	tail (toil)	fail (foil)
jay (joy)	nose (noise)	tea (toy)	cone (coin)

DICTATION AND WRITING Have children number a sheet of paper 1–8. Write *boil* on the board, and tell children that in the words you will say, /oi/ will be spelled *oi* as in *boil*. Dictate the words, and have children write them. After they write each word, write the words on the board so children can proofread their work. Have them draw a line through a misspelled word and write the correct spelling below it.

1. soil	2. coin	3. point*	4. spoil*	*Word appears in "When You Visit Relatives."*
5. join*	6. foil	7. moist	8. oil	

Tell children that in the following sentences, /oi/ is spelled *oy*. Dictate these sentences: *Roy is a boy. Joy is a girl. Roy and Joy play with toys.*

READ LONGER WORDS *Vowel Diphthongs* Write the word *enjoy* on the board. Tell children that they can often figure out longer words by looking for word parts they know. Ask which part of the word says *en* and which part of the word says *joy*. Then ask what the whole word says. Follow a similar procedure to have children read the words *joyful, enjoyment,* and *loyal*.

REPRODUCIBLE STUDENT ACTIVITY PAGE
....
INDEPENDENT PRACTICE See the reproducible Student Activity on page 159.

Name _____

When You Visit Relatives

Write the word that makes the sentence tell about the picture.

1. Roy is a tall _____.

           oil   boy   bee

2. I put the _____ away.

         coin   boy   join

3. The water starts to _____.

         point   boil   boat

4. Joy will _____ the softball team.

         coil   jog   join

5. I plant seeds in the _____.

         soil   seal   spoil

6. This train is a fun _____.

         join   top   toy

7. That bird makes a lot of _____.

         boys   coins   noise

Harcourt

Introducing Vocabulary

bicycle	a vehicle that has two wheels and pedals
forget	opposite of *remember*; to fail to do something
remember	opposite of *forget*; to keep in mind
travel	to go from one place to another
weather	kind of day it is outside, such as hot, sunny, rainy, and windy
wheels	informal word for *bikes*

Apply word identification strategies.

IDENTIFY VOCABULARY WORDS Display the vocabulary words, and ask children to identify the ones they know. Remind children that they can sometimes figure out an unfamiliar word by thinking about spelling patterns, letter patterns, smaller words, and word parts. If necessary, help children find the smaller words or word parts to help them read *forget, remember,* and *travel.* (*for/get; re/mem/ber; trav/el*) Ask what spelling or letter patterns helped them read the words. (*or*; CVC; *er*) Then point out the CVVC pattern to help children read *wheels.* Finally, point to and read aloud *bicycle* and *weather.* Have children read them aloud after you.

Check understanding.

Discuss the meanings of the vocabulary words. Then ask children to write the vocabulary words on a sheet of paper. Have them name the word that answers each of the following questions and circle that word on their papers.

> Which word . . .
>
> - **tells what you do when you go on a trip?** *(travel)*
> - **names what rain, wind, sunshine, and snow are?** *(weather)*
> - **means "to keep in mind"?** *(remember)*
> - **is the opposite of *remember?*** *(forget)*
> - **names something you can ride?** *(bicycle)*
> - **is another word for *bikes*?** *(wheels)*

Some children may be unfamiliar with the words in the title of the selection that they will read. After distributing the vocabulary page, point to the title, "When You Visit Relatives," read it aloud, and have children say it with you.

REPRODUCIBLE STUDENT ACTIVITY PAGE

INDEPENDENT PRACTICE See the reproducible Student Activity on page 161.

NOTE: The following vocabulary words from "Dinosaurs Travel" are reinforced in "When You Visit Relatives." If children are unfamiliar with these words, point them out as you encounter them during reading: *relatives* (p. 214); *companion* (p. 215); *luggage, sturdy* (p. 217); and *cassette* (p. 218).

When You Visit Relatives

Read the story.

I will visit my aunt.
I love to <u>travel</u>!

I won't <u>forget</u> my
toothbrush.

I must <u>remember</u> to
tell my aunt I am
on my way.

I ride my <u>bicycle</u> to
my aunt's house.

I wish the <u>weather</u>
was better.

Those <u>wheels</u> would
be better today.

Write a story word to complete each sentence. Choose from the underlined words above.

1. Ernest likes to _____ and see new places.

2. Ernest could have taken a train, but he rode his _____.

3. The _____ was not very good for a bike ride.

4. Ernest hoped his _____ wouldn't slip in the rain.

5. He tried to _____ to pack everything for the trip.

6. He didn't want to _____ anything!

Directed Reading

Read aloud the title of the story. Ask children to name some *relatives* that they might like to visit. Then have children read page 214 to find out what to do before visiting relatives. **What should you do before you visit relatives?** (*Call them.*) INFERENTIAL: SEQUENCE **Why should you call first?** (*to give your relatives time to get ready for company*) INFERENTIAL: CAUSE AND EFFECT **Why do you think you should get a present?** (Responses will vary.) CRITICAL: OFFER OPINIONS

Page 215 Have children look at the illustration on page 215. Then read aloud the heading. Have children read to find out why you might ask a companion to join you. **Why might you ask a companion to join you?** (*so you will not have to travel alone*) LITERAL: CAUSE AND EFFECT **What must you do first?** (*You must ask your relatives if it's okay.*) LITERAL: SEQUENCE

Page 216 Read aloud the heading. Then have children read page 216 to find out what "those wheels" are. **What are "those wheels"?** (*a bicycle*) INFERENTIAL: USE CONTEXT CLUES **What should you do if you are biking?** (*Bike in good weather; don't bike too far; avoid traffic; travel on safe roads; bring snacks.*) INFERENTIAL: INTERPRET STORY EVENTS/SUMMARIZE

Page 217 Have children read aloud the heading on page 217. Ask children what luggage is. Then have them read page 217 to find out what to pack for a trip. **What should you pack for a trip?** (*clothes, toys, and a raincoat*) LITERAL: NOTE DETAILS

Page 218 Have children read aloud the heading on page 218. Then have them read the page to find out what rules to follow. **What rules should you follow when you visit?** (*Carry your luggage; wipe your feet; don't play loud music; don't jump on the bed; don't eat in bed; be quiet; don't stay too long.*) LITERAL: NOTE DETAILS **Which rule does the author think is most important? How do you know?** (*"Don't stay too long!" It is printed in capital letters, and it is followed by an exclamation point.*) METACOGNITIVE: AUTHOR'S PURPOSE **Which rule do *you* think is most important? Why?** (Responses will vary.) CRITICAL: MAKE JUDGMENTS

Page 219 Have children read aloud the heading on page 219. Then have them read page 219 to learn how to help out. **What are some ways to help out?** (*Make your bed; pick up your toys; make lunch; wash the dishes.*) LITERAL: NOTE DETAILS **What other things might you do to help out?** (Responses will vary.) CRITICAL: EXTEND THE STORY

Page 220 Have children read the heading on page 220. Then have them read the page to find out how to thank their relatives. **What are some ways to say *thank you*?** (*Tell your relatives that you had a good time; thank them for having you; invite them to visit you; send a thank-you note.*) LITERAL: NOTE DETAILS

SUMMARIZING THE SELECTION Ask children to recall the tips that they read about in this selection. Then help them summarize the selection in a few sentences.

Answers to Think About It Questions

Page 221 1. First, you should call and tell your relatives about your travel plans. When you are there, you should follow the rules and help out. SUMMARY
2. A raincoat can keep you dry, and dry travelers are happy travelers. INTERPRETATION
3. Accept reasonable responses. TASK

Name _____

When You Visit Relatives

Write *beginning*, *middle*, or *end* under each picture to show the order of events in "When You Visit Relatives."

_____   _____   _____

Now use the words in the boxes to answer the questions.

Beginning	**relatives travel**

What does Ernest want to do? _____

_____

Middle	**bicycle weather forgets**

What is Ernest's trip like? _____

_____

What happens at his relatives' house?   **helps   broke**

_____

End	**note relatives**

What does Ernest remember to do at the end of his visit?

_____

Harcourt

If I Could Fly

by Deborah Akers   **Use with *Blue Skies*, pages 222–229.**

Preteaching Skills: Vowel Variants /ŏŏ/oo; /ōō/oo

Teach/Model

IDENTIFY THE SOUND Ask children to repeat the following sentence several times: *The kangaroo at the zoo stood on the wood at noon.* Ask which words in the sentence have the /ŏŏ/ sound that children hear in *hood.* (*stood, wood*) Then ask which words have the /ōō/ sound that children hear in *food.* (*kangaroo, zoo, noon*)

ASSOCIATE LETTERS TO THEIR SOUNDS On the board, write the sentence *The kangaroo at the zoo stood on the wood at noon.* Circle the words *stood* and *wood,* and ask how these two words are alike. (*same vowel sound; letters* oo) Underline the letters *oo* in *stood* and *wood.* Tell children that when the letters *oo* come together in a word, they sometimes stand for the /ŏŏ/ sound that children hear in *stood* and *wood.* Remind children that sometimes the same letter or letters can stand for different sounds. Then follow a similar procedure to introduce the letters *oo* and the /ōō/ sound in the words *kangaroo, zoo,* and *noon.*

WORD BLENDING Write *pool* on the board. Model blending the sounds to read *pool.* Slide your hand under the word as you slowly elongate the sounds /ppōōll/. Then read the word *pool* naturally. Have children practice blending sounds to read aloud these words: *hook, stool, broom, brook.* Emphasize the importance of trying a different sound for *oo* if a word does not sound right at first.

Practice/Apply

APPLY THE SKILL *Vowel Substitution* Write the first word in each pair of words below on the board, and have children read it aloud. Make the changes necessary to form each word in parentheses. Have children read each new word.

coal (cool)	goal (good)	roaster (rooster)	feet (foot)
pail (pool)	shake (shook)	boat (boot)	had (hood)

DICTATION AND WRITING Have children number a sheet of paper 1–8. Dictate the following words, and have children write them. After they write each word, write it on the board so children can proofread their work. Have them draw a line through a misspelled word and write the correct spelling below it.

1. cook*	2. boot	3. soon	4. book*	*Word appears in
5. hoof	6. pool	7. cool	8. shook	"If I Could Fly."

Dictate the following sentences: *I sit on the stool in my room. I look at my book. It tells me how to cook food.*

READ LONGER WORDS *Compound Words* Write the word *cookbook* on the board. Tell children that they can often figure out longer words by looking for words they know in them. Cover the word *book,* and have children read the word that is left. Follow a similar procedure to have children read the word *book.* Then blend the two smaller words to read aloud the longer word *cookbook.* Follow a similar procedure to have children blend smaller words to read these compound words: *bedroom, broomstick, noontime.*

REPRODUCIBLE STUDENT ACTIVITY PAGE

INDEPENDENT PRACTICE See the reproducible Student Activity on page 165.

If I Could Fly

Fill in the oval in front of the sentence that tells about the picture.

1 ◯ Sue put the ball in the pool.
   ◯ The ball went in the hoop.
   ◯ Sue stood on the book.

2 ◯ The robin makes a loop.
   ◯ The bird is at the zoo.
   ◯ The bird flies in front of the moon.

3 ◯ Nate shook the fruit down.
   ◯ Nate waded in the brook.
   ◯ Nate stood on a stool.

4 ◯ Lew gives the book to Sue.
   ◯ Lew has a new cookbook.
   ◯ Lew likes his new boots.

5 ◯ My boots are in that room.
   ◯ We will go to the pool soon.
   ◯ There is a toolbox on the roof.

6 ◯ Dan looks for his blue shoe.
   ◯ He cooks a good stew.
   ◯ The boy hooks a fish in the brook.

Harcourt

Introducing Vocabulary

Apply word identification strategies.

IDENTIFY VOCABULARY WORDS Display the vocabulary words, and ask children to identify the ones they know. Remind children that they can sometimes figure out an unfamiliar word by thinking about spelling patterns, letter patterns, smaller words, and word parts. Have children find the smaller words to help them read *grandma*. (*grand/ma*) Ask what spelling pattern helped them read the word. (*CVC*) Then point to and read aloud each of the other vocabulary words. Have children read them aloud after you.

Check understanding.

Discuss the meanings of the vocabulary words. Then have children write the vocabulary words on a sheet of paper. Have them name the word that answers each of the following questions and circle that word on their papers.

VOCABULARY DEFINED

adventure a fun, exciting experience

buildings structures built by people, such as houses, factories, or schools

city a large town

country a nation; all of the land that makes up a nation

grandma grandmother; a child's parent's mother

people men, women, and children; human beings

Which word...

- **is another word for a nation?** *(country)*
- **names a large town where many people live?** *(city)*
- **completes this sentence:** *Is my ___ my mother's mother?* *(grandma)*
- **tells what a house and a library are?** *(buildings)*
- **tells what men, women, and children are?** *(people)*
- **means "an exciting experience"?** *(adventure)*

REPRODUCIBLE STUDENT ACTIVITY PAGE

INDEPENDENT PRACTICE See the reproducible Student Activity on page 167.

NOTE: The following vocabulary words from "Abuela" are reinforced in "If I Could Fly." If children are unfamiliar with these words, point them out as you encounter them during reading: *glide* (p. 222); *soared* (p. 223); *flock, harbor,* and *swooping* (p. 224).

Name _____

If I Could Fly

Write a word from the box to complete each sentence.

country	people	buildings	city	grandma	adventure

"What an _____ we could have if we could fly!" said Luke.	"We could fly over a big _____ like New York," June said.	"We could fly over tall _____," Sally said.
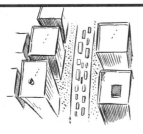 "The _____ would look as small as bugs down there!" said Luke.	 "We could fly to a new _____," they said.	 "I could visit my _____!" they all shouted.

Read the story to find out about the kids' adventure!

Harcourt

Directed Reading

Page 222 Read aloud the title on page 222. Ask children how they would finish the sentence *If I could fly, . . .* Then have children read page 222 to find out where Luke would fly. **Where would Luke go if he could fly?** (*to the city*) LITERAL: NOTE DETAILS **If Luke could fly, what would he do like a plane and like a bird?** (*He would take off like a plane and glide like a bird.*) LITERAL: NOTE DETAILS

Page 223 Have children read page 223 to find out what Luke would do in the city. **What does Luke mean when he says he "would sail over the buildings"?** (Possible response: *He would fly high up in the sky over the city.*) INFERENTIAL: UNDERSTAND FIGURATIVE LANGUAGE **Why would Luke look into store windows?** (*He would want to see all the best toys.*) INFERENTIAL: UNDERSTAND CHARACTERS' MOTIVATION **Why might Luke think that flying over the city would be the best adventure?** (Accept reasonable responses.) INFERENTIAL: SPECULATE

Page 224 Have children look at the illustration to predict where June would fly. Then have them read page 224 to confirm their predictions. **Where would June go if she could fly?** (*She would fly to a country where people love to play.*) LITERAL: NOTE DETAILS

Page 225 Have children read page 225 to find out what June would do in that country. **Would June teach people to fly?** (*yes*) INFERENTIAL: INTERPRET STORY EVENTS **What would June and her new friends do?** (*They would have a big party in the sky, eat cake, and dance on the clouds.*) LITERAL: NOTE DETAILS **What do you think Sally would like to do if she could fly?** (Accept reasonable responses.) CRITICAL: MAKE PREDICTIONS

Page 226 Have children read page 226 to find out where Sally would go if she could fly. **Where would Sally go if she could fly? Why?** (*She would go visit her grandma because her grandma moved far away, and Sally misses her.*) INFERENTIAL: UNDERSTAND CHARACTERS' MOTIVES

Page 227 Have children read page 227 to find out what Sally would do with her grandma after they ate. **What would Sally do with her grandma?** (*She would take a walk, go fishing, look for whales, watch the sun go down, and read with her.*) INFERENTIAL: SUMMARIZE **How is Sally's adventure like Luke's and June's? How is it different?** (Possible response: *The adventures are alike because the children would all fly. Sally's is different because it could happen in real life. The others do something make-believe.*) INFERENTIAL: COMPARE AND CONTRAST **Why would Sally's adventure be the best for her?** (Accept reasonable responses.) CRITICAL: UNDERSTAND CHARACTERS' FEELINGS

SUMMARIZING THE SELECTION Ask children to think about what Luke, June, and Sally would do if they could fly. Help children briefly summarize the story.

Answers to Think About It Questions

Page 228 1. Luke would fly over a big city; June would fly to a place where people love to play; Sally would fly to visit her grandma, who has moved far away. SUMMARY
2. Sally loves her grandma. I can tell because Sally misses her grandma, would go to visit her grandma, and would do a lot of fun things with her grandma. INTERPRETATION
3. Accept reasonable responses. TASK

Page 229 For instruction on the Focus Skill: Word Endings, see page 229 in *Blue Skies*.

If I Could Fly

Read the clues. Then complete the puzzle with words from the box.

| country | adventure | grandma | city | buildings | people |

Across

3. Luke wanted to look into the windows of _____.

6. June said she wanted to go to a new _____.

Down

1. Luke wanted to go to a _____.

2. Luke told his friends he would have the best _____.

4. Sally said she wanted to visit her _____.

5. June said she wanted to find a place where _____ play all the time.

On another sheet of paper, write the completed clues. Write a number in front of each sentence to show the order of events in the story.

Phonics

An Amazing Feat

by Susan M. Fischer   **Use with *Blue Skies*, pages 230–237.**

Preteaching Skills: Consonant /s/ce, ci, cy

Teach/Model

IDENTIFY THE SOUND Have children repeat the following sentence aloud several times: *The city mice are in the center of an icy place.* Ask children to tell which words in the sentence have the /s/ sound. (*city, mice, center, icy, place*)

ASSOCIATE LETTERS TO THEIR SOUNDS On the board, write the sentence *The city mice are in the center of an icy place.* Circle the words *city, mice, center, icy,* and *place,* and ask how these words are alike. (*All have the /s/ sound; all have the letter c.*) Underline the letters *ci* in *city.* Remind children that sometimes the same letter or letters can stand for different sounds. Then tell children that when the letter *c* is followed by an *i,* it often stands for the /s/ sound that children hear in *city.* Follow a similar procedure with the letters *ce* in *mice, center,* and *place,* and with *cy* in *icy.*

WORD BLENDING Write *face* on the board. Model blending the sounds to read *face.* Slide your hand under the word as you slowly elongate the sounds. Then read the word naturally. Have children practice blending sounds to read aloud these words: *space, circle, rice.* For *circle,* point out the different sounds for *c.*

Practice/Apply

APPLY THE SKILL *Consonant Substitution* Write the first word in each pair of words on the board, and have children read it aloud. Make the changes necessary to form each word in parentheses. Ask children to read the new words.

bell (cell)	lent (cent)	rake (race)	ride (rice)
spine (spice)	Mike (mice)	spider (cider)	trade (trace)

DICTATION AND WRITING Have children number a sheet of paper 1–8. Tell them that in the words you say, the /s/ sound is spelled with a *c.* Dictate the following words, and have children write them. After they have finished, write each word on the board so children can proofread their work. Have them draw a line through a misspelled word and write the correct spelling above it.

1. rice	2. chance	3. trace	4. place*	*Word appears in
5. circle	6. decided*	7. center*	8. city*	"An Amazing Feat."

Dictate the following sentence: *The nice mice eat rice in the city.*

READ LONGER WORDS *Closed CVC* Write the word *celery* on the board. Remind children that they can often figure out longer words by looking for word parts they know in them. Ask children which part of the word says *cel,* which part says *er,* and which part says *y.* Then ask what *cel, er,* and *y* together say. (*celery*) Explain that in longer words with CVC patterns, like *celery,* children might have to try both the long and short sounds for the vowel to see which one sounds correct. Then follow a similar procedure to have children blend word parts to read these longer words: *palace, civil, celebrate.*

REPRODUCIBLE STUDENT ACTIVITY PAGE

INDEPENDENT PRACTICE See the reproducible Student Activity on page 171.

Name _____

An Amazing Feat

Read the story. Circle all the words with _c_ that have the sound you hear in _city_.

The Race

Today is the bicycle race in Cedar City. The race goes in a big circle around Cash Park. Kim finds a space at the starting line. He ties his shoelaces. He puts on his nice new helmet. Then the race begins. The wind in Kim's face is cool. After the race, Kim drinks some juice. He didn't win, but he still celebrates with his mom and dad.

Choose from the words you circled to complete each sentence.

1. There is a bicycle _____ today.

2. The race is in Cedar _____.

3. The race goes in a big _____ around the park.

4. Kim feels the wind on his _____.

5. He drinks _____ after the race.

6. He _____ with his mom and dad.

Harcourt

Introducing Vocabulary

IDENTIFY VOCABULARY WORDS Display the
vocabulary words, and ask children to identify the
ones they know. Remind children that they can
sometimes figure out an unfamiliar word by looking for spelling patterns, letter patterns, smaller
words, and word parts they know. Have children
use the CVC spelling pattern and the sounds for
the letters *or* to help them read *records.* Then
point to and read aloud each of the other vocabulary words. (*disappeared, engines, fuel, gasoline,
weight*) Have children read them aloud after you.

**Check
understanding.**

Discuss the meanings of the vocabulary words.
Then ask children to write the vocabulary words
on a sheet of paper. Have children name the word
that answers each of the following questions and
circle that word on their papers.

VOCABULARY DEFINED

disappeared passed from
sight; vanished

engines machines that use
energy to make things—like
cars or airplanes—work or
move

fuel something that is burned
to make heat or power, such
as wood, coal, or oil

gasoline a liquid fuel that is
made from oil

records the highest scores or
fastest speeds ever; the best
yet done

weight the heaviness of the
load that is carried

Which word . . .

- **names the heaviness of something you are carrying?** *(weight)*
- **tells what things turn on when cars are started?** *(engines)*
- **tells what runners try to set by going very fast?** *(records)*
- **names what you put in your car at the pump of a gas station?**
  (gasoline)
- **best completes this sentence?** *The mice ___ when the cat came in.*
  (disappeared)
- **tells what oil, wood, coal, and gas all can be?** *(fuel)*

Some children may be unfamiliar with some of the words in the title of the
selection that they will read. Read aloud the title, "An Amazing Feat," and have
children read it with you. Explain that a feat is an accomplishment or an action
that is special in some way.

**REPRODUCIBLE
STUDENT
ACTIVITY PAGE**

**INDEPENDENT
PRACTICE** See
the reproducible
Student Activity
on page 173.

NOTE: The following vocabulary words from "Ruth Law Thrills a Nation" are
reinforced in "An Amazing Feat." If children are unfamiliar with these words,
point them out as you encounter them during reading: *heroine, refused* (p. 230);
feat, spectators, and *hospitality* (p. 233).

An Amazing Feat

Read the story. Then fill in the web. Use all the underlined words in your answers.

Long ago, a little girl went to a fair. She saw an airplane for the first time. She listened to the <u>engines</u> roar. She smelled the <u>gasoline</u> in the tanks. She gazed as the beautiful plane <u>disappeared</u> into the sky. She had many questions about planes. How much <u>weight</u> could it carry? How much <u>fuel</u> did it need?

That girl was Amelia Earhart. When she grew up, she set many flying <u>records</u>. Learn more about Amelia Earhart in the story.

What did she see the beautiful plane do?

disappeared
_____

What did she hear at the fair?

engines
_____

Amelia Earhart

What questions did she have about planes?

Responses should
include the words
weight and fuel.

What did she set when she grew up?

records
_____

What did she smell at the fair?

gasoline
_____

Directed Reading

Page 230   Read aloud the title on page 230. Ask children what amazing feats they or people they know about have accomplished. Explain that this selection is about the amazing feats of a woman named Amelia Earhart. Then have children read page 230 to find out about Amelia Earhart. **Who was Amelia Earhart?** (*an American heroine; a pilot*) LITERAL: NOTE DETAILS   **What type of person do you think Amelia Earhart was? Why?** (Possible response: *She was brave and independent. I think this because she was a pilot when there weren't many women pilots and because once she decided to do something, she always followed through.*) CRITICAL: UNDERSTAND CHARACTERS' TRAITS

Page 231   Have children read page 231 to find out when Amelia Earhart fell in love with airplanes. **When did Amelia Earhart fall in love with planes?** (*when she was eleven and saw an airplane at a fair*) LITERAL: NOTE DETAILS   **What did Amelia Earhart do during the war?** (*She was a nurse; she watched the pilots and their airplanes.*) LITERAL: SEQUENCE **What did she decide to do after the war?** (*fly airplanes herself*) LITERAL: SEQUENCE

Page 232   Have children read page 232. Ask: **What did Amelia do after the war?** (*She took flying lessons and got her own plane.*) LITERAL: SEQUENCE   **What did Amelia do in the Friendship?** (*She flew higher than any woman had flown.*) LITERAL: NOTE DETAILS

Page 233   Have children read page 233 to find out about some of Amelia Earhart's feats. **What were some of Amelia's feats?** (*She flew across the Atlantic Ocean alone; she set records for speed and distance.*) INFERENTIAL: SUMMARIZE   **Why do you think spectators came to cheer for Amelia?** (Possible responses: *She was a famous pilot; people liked her; she was making history.*) CRITICAL: SPECULATE   **What is hospitality?** (*friendly treatment to guests or visitors*) INFERENTIAL: USE CONTEXT CLUES

Page 234   Read aloud the first sentence of page 234. Ask children what they think Amelia's dream was. Then have them read page 234 to find out. **What was Amelia's dream?** (*to fly all the way around the world*) LITERAL: NOTE DETAILS   **Why do you think this would be an even more amazing feat?** (Responses will vary.) CRITICAL: SPECULATE   **Why did Amelia want to take Fred Noonan on her long trip?** (*to help her on such a long trip*) INFERENTIAL: UNDERSTAND CHARACTERS' MOTIVES

Page 235   Have children read page 235. Ask: **What did Amelia and Fred do before they left?** (*They filled the tanks with gasoline and checked the engine.*) INFERENTIAL: SEQUENCE **What happened to the plane?** (*It ran out of fuel and disappeared.*) LITERAL: NOTE DETAILS

Page 236   Read aloud page 236. Then ask children what they think Amelia Earhart meant when she said, "The dreams of long ago had come true." Model a response as necessary: **Long ago, people could only dream of flying, but now they could actually fly. I think Amelia was telling people that if they tried hard enough, in time they could make other dreams become realities.**

SUMMARIZING THE SELECTION Ask children to think about what they learned about the beginning, the middle, and the end of Amelia Earhart's life. Then help them summarize the selection in three or four sentences.

Answers to Think About It Questions

Page 237   1. She was a pilot who was courageous and who set many flying records. SUMMARY
2. The partner could look at the maps, help fly, or be good company. INTERPRETATION
3. Accept reasonable responses. TASK

Name _____

An Amazing Feat

Complete the chart to tell about the story.

Cause		Effect	
Amelia went to a fair. She listened to the roar of the _____.	→	She decided she wanted to be a _____.	
engines lion train		**teacher trainer pilot**	
Amelia worked hard to pay for lessons and _____.	→	She flew to places all over the _____.	
food gasoline toys		**river world fair**	
Amelia was very _____.	→	She broke many flying _____.	
brave sad sorry		**dish plane records**	

Answer these questions to tell about the rest of the story.

1. What brave thing did Amelia want to do when she was 40?

   _____

   _____

2. What was her plane filled with? _____

3. What happened to Amelia on this flight? _____

   _____

4. If you could meet Amelia Earhart, what would you ask her?

   _____

Harcourt

Phonics

Space Trip

by Caren B. Stelson   **Use with *Blue Skies*, pages 238–245.**

Preteaching Skills: Vowel Variants /ô/aw, au(gh)

Teach/Model

IDENTIFY THE SOUND Ask children to repeat the following sentence several times: *Paul caught his puppy crawling on the lawn.* Have children tell which words in the sentence have the /ô/ sound. (*Paul, caught, crawling, lawn*)

ASSOCIATE LETTERS TO THEIR SOUNDS On the board, write the sentence *Paul caught his puppy crawling on the lawn.* Circle the words *Paul* and *caught*, and ask how these words are alike. (*the /ô/ sound; the letters* au) Underline the letters *au* in *Paul* and the letters *augh* in *caught*. Tell children that when these letters come together in a word, they usually stand for the /ô/ sound that children hear in *Paul* and *caught*. Follow a similar procedure with the letters *aw* in *crawling* and *lawn*.

WORD BLENDING Write *taught* on the board. Model blending the sounds to read *taught*. Slide your hand under the word as you slowly elongate the sounds. Then read the word *taught* naturally. Have children practice blending sounds to read aloud these words: *pause, claws, daughter, fawn.*

Practice/Apply

APPLY THE SKILL *Vowel Substitution* Write the first word in each of the following word pairs on the board, and have children read it aloud. Then make the changes necessary to form each word in parentheses. Have children read each new word.

jay (jaw)   lay (law)   pay (paw)   hail (haul)
pail (Paul)   stray (straw) cat (caught)   fern (fawn)

DICTATION AND WRITING Have children number a sheet of paper 1–8. Write the word *law* on the board, and tell children that in the words you will say, the /ô/ sound is spelled *aw*. Dictate the words, and have children write them. After they have finished, write each word on the board so children can proofread their work. Have them draw a line through a misspelled word and write the correct spelling above it.

1. raw   2. straw   3. jaw   4. dawn*   *Word appears in
5. crawl*   6. law*   7. fawn   8. hawk   "Space Trip."*

Tell children that in these sentences, /ô/ is spelled *au*. Dictate the following sentences: *Paul hauls these to the launch pad. Then he pauses. What is the cause for his pause?*

READ LONGER WORDS *Compound Words* Write the word *because* on the board. Remind children that they can often figure out longer words by looking for smaller words in them. Cover the word *cause*, and have children read the word that is left. Follow a similar procedure to have children read the word *cause*. Then blend the two word parts to read aloud the longer word *because*. Follow a similar procedure to have children blend the smaller words to read these longer words: *granddaughter, strawberry, seesaw.*

REPRODUCIBLE STUDENT ACTIVITY PAGE
. . . .
INDEPENDENT PRACTICE See the reproducible Student Activity on page 177.

Space Trip

Do what the sentences tell you.

1. Do you see the baby crawling? Color his shirt yellow.
2. Can you find the hawk? Draw a tree for it to perch on.
3. Color the lawn green.
4. Do you see someone yawning? Color her shirt blue.
5. Find the fawn and circle it. Color it brown.
6. Shauna has pasta with sauce for lunch. Color the sauce red.
7. Draw some clouds in the sky.
8. Can you see the dog? Color him black with white paws.

Circle the words with the vowel sound you hear in _saw._

Harcourt

Introducing Vocabulary

Apply word identification strategies.

IDENTIFY VOCABULARY WORDS Display the vocabulary words, and ask children to identify the ones they know. Remind children that they can sometimes figure out an unfamiliar word by thinking about spelling patterns, letter patterns, smaller words, and word parts. Have children use the CVC*e* pattern to help them read aloud *write* and *rotates*. Have them look for smaller words in *orbit* and *postcards*. Then have them look for the word parts in *universe* (*uni/verse*) and *liquid* (*li/quid*) to read aloud each of those words.

Check understanding.

Discuss the meanings of the vocabulary words. Then ask children to write the vocabulary words on a sheet of paper. Have them name the word that answers each of the following questions and circle that word on their papers.

VOCABULARY DEFINED
liquid water, milk, or juice; a substance that flows like water
orbit to travel around something
postcards cards used for sending a message by mail
rotates spins; turns in a circle
universe everything there is; the entire world including outer space
write to make marks, letters, words, or numbers with a pen or pencil

Which word. . .

- **tells what planets do around the sun?** *(orbit)*
- **tells what a tire on a car does when it turns?** *(rotates)*
- **names things that you can send in the mail?** *(postcards)*
- **means "to make letters and words on paper"?** *(write)*
- **names the whole world and more, including outer space?** *(universe)*
- **names something that you can swim in?** *(liquid)*

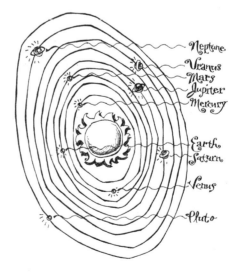

REPRODUCIBLE STUDENT ACTIVITY PAGE

INDEPENDENT PRACTICE See the reproducible Student Activity on page 179.

NOTE: The following vocabulary words from "Postcards from Pluto" are reinforced in "Space Trip." If children are unfamiliar with these words, point them out as you encounter them during reading: *guide* (p. 238); *surface, lightning* (p. 239); *assemble, intense, dangerous* (p. 240); and *reflects* (p. 243).

Space Trip

Write a word from the box to complete each sentence.

write	rotates	postcards	liquid	universe	orbit

These kids are going on a space trip to find out about our _____.

They will find out that the surface of our planet is mostly _____.

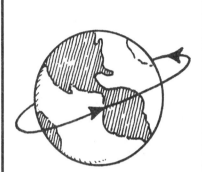

They will find out that our planet _____, or spins around.

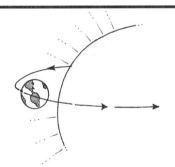

They will find out that it takes our planet one year to _____ the sun.

They will _____ about their trip.

Maybe they will even send some _____ home.

Directed Reading

Pages 238–239 Ask children to read aloud the title on page 238. Ask children what they might learn on a space trip. Then have children read pages 238–239 to find out about the space trip. **What does *launch* mean?** (*take off; blast off; go up*) INFERENTIAL: USE CONTEXT CLUES   **Why is Earth called the blue planet?** (*Most of its surface is covered with water.*) INFERENTIAL: CAUSE AND EFFECT   **What are the brown and green places?** (*land*) LITERAL: NOTE DETAILS

Pages 240–241 Read aloud the first two sentences on page 240. Ask children what they think they will see on Earth. Then have them read page 240 to find out. **What do you think a Space Scope is?** (Possible response: *something like a telescope to see things close up*) INFERENTIAL: DRAW CONCLUSIONS   **What do the space travelers see on Earth?** (*people, animals, and plants*) LITERAL: NOTE DETAILS   **Why can't we live on the other planets?** (*They are either too hot or too cold.*) INFERENTIAL: CAUSE AND EFFECT

Pages 242–243 Read aloud the first two sentences on page 243. Have children read the first paragraph to find out what happens as Earth spins. **How long does it take Earth to rotate once?** (*24 hours*) LITERAL: NOTE DETAILS   **What causes night and day?** (Possible response: *As Earth rotates, the part that faces the sun has day, and the other part has night.*) INFERENTIAL: CAUSE AND EFFECT   Have children read the second paragraph on page 243 to find out about how long it takes Earth to orbit the sun. **How long does it take Earth to orbit the sun?** (*one year*) LITERAL: NOTE DETAILS   **How fast does Earth move?** (*67,000 miles an hour*) LITERAL: NOTE DETAILS

Page 244 Have children read page 244 to find out where the travelers are about to land. **Where are the space travelers landing?** (*on Earth's moon*) LITERAL: NOTE DETAILS **How far is Earth from its moon?** (*240,000 miles*) LITERAL: NOTE DETAILS   **How is Earth's moon different from Earth?** (Possible response: *There is no air or liquid on the moon.*) INFERENTIAL: COMPARE AND CONTRAST   **Do you think there is really a gift shop on the moon?** (*no*) **When do you think this story takes place?** (*sometime in the future*) INFERENTIAL: SPECULATE/DRAW CONCLUSIONS

SUMMARIZING THE SELECTION Ask children to think about the Space Trip Ship's tour. Then help them summarize the information they learned on the tour. (Possible response: *Earth is the third planet from the sun. It is the only known planet on which people, plants, and animals can live, because it is the right temperature and has air and water. Earth rotates and that is why there is night and day. Earth also orbits the sun. Earth has one moon that is about 240,000 miles away from it.*) INFERENTIAL: SUMMARIZE

Answers to Think About It Questions

Page 245 1. Most of Earth's surface is liquid; Earth is the only planet we know of on which people, animals, and plants can live; Earth rotates and that gives us night and day; it takes one year for Earth to orbit the sun; Earth's moon is about 240,000 miles away. SUMMARY
2. It is too hot on the planets closer to the sun. INTERPRETATION
3. Accept reasonable responses. TASK

Name _____

 Space Trip

Complete the story strip with facts you learned in "Space Trip."

What planet did the kids see? _____ Earth _____ _____ _____	Why is Earth called the blue planet? Most of Earth's surface is water.	What are the brown and green places on Earth? _____ land _____ _____ _____
How long does it take for Earth to orbit the sun once? _____ one year _____ _____ _____	How long does it take for Earth to rotate once? _____ 24 hours _____ _____ _____	Which is bigger, the universe or Earth? _____ the universe _____ _____ _____
What did the kids write when they were on the moon? _____ postcards _____ _____ _____	What would you like to see on a space trip? Why? Responses will vary. _____ _____	

Harcourt

Index

Consonants

Digraphs

Diphthongs

Long Vowels

R-Controlled Vowels

Short Vowels

Vowel Variants

DATE DUE

~~DEC 1 8 2012~~			
~~AUG 1 3 2013~~			
~~DEC 1 8 2014~~			
~~AUG 1 7 2015~~			

Demco, Inc. 38-293

Introducing Vocabulary

**Apply word
identification
strategies.**

IDENTIFY VOCABULARY WORDS Display the
vocabulary words, and ask children to identify
the ones they know. Remind children that they
can sometimes figure out an unfamiliar word by
looking for familiar spelling or letter patterns.
Point out the CVC pattern in *end* and *wind*. Ask
children to use what they know about the CVC
pattern to help them read these words. Follow a
similar procedure with *or* and the word *morning*.
Then have children find the two smaller words to
help them read the longer word *today*.

Point to *beginning* and *tomorrow* in turn, and read each word aloud. Have children
read it aloud after you.

VOCABULARY DEFINED	
beginning	starting
end	the last part
morning	the first part of the day; from sunrise to noon
today	this day
tomorrow	the next day
wind	air that is blowing

**Check
understanding.**

Discuss the meanings of the vocabulary words. Then ask children to write the
vocabulary words on a sheet of paper. Have children name the word that completes
each of the following sentences and circle it on their papers.

- **I wake up at 7:00 in the ___.** *(morning)*
- **When something is starting, it is ___.** *(beginning)*
- **A story is over at the ___.** *(end)*
- **I will go the day after this one. I will go ___.** *(tomorrow)*
- **I must work on this day. I must work ___.** *(today)*
- **The ___ blew my hat away.** *(wind)*

Children may be unfamiliar with some of the words in the title of the selection
that they will read. After distributing the vocabulary page, point to the title,
"While the Bear Sleeps," read it aloud, and have children read it with you.

**REPRODUCIBLE
STUDENT
ACTIVITY PAGE**

**INDEPENDENT
PRACTICE** See
the reproducible
Student Activity
on page 83.

NOTE: The following vocabulary words from "When the Wind Stops" are reinforced in "While the Bear Sleeps." If children are unfamiliar with these words,
point them out as you encounter them during reading: *autumn* (p. 110); *dusky,
glowing, pointed* (p. 111); *completely* (p. 114); and *sliver* (p. 115).

Name _____

While the Bear Sleeps

Read the story. Circle the words with *er*, *ir*, or *ur*.

A bird and a turtle met one day. "I can surf!" the turtle said.

"Well, I can fly," said the bird. "Let's go up to my perch."

"Let's go surfing," said the turtle. "No thanks," said the bird. "I do not want to surf. I will get my shirt wet."

"As you like," said the turtle. "Now, will you get me back on firm ground? This perch is too far up for a turtle."

Circle the word to complete each sentence. Write it on the line.

1. A _____ and a turtle met one day.
  third   bird   perfect

2. The bird took the turtle to its _____ .
  surf   perch   turn

3. The bird did not want to get its _____ wet.
  shirt   perch   dirt

4. The turtle wanted to get back on _____ ground.
  firm   term   first